HOW TO GET A JOB AND KEEP IT BY LETTING THE HOLY SPIRIT WORK FOR YOU

By Gilbert M. Miller

HOW TO GET A JOB AND KEEP IT BY LETTING THE HOLY SPIRIT WORK FOR YOU
by Gilbert M. Miller

Printed in the United States of America

ISBN-13: 978-1-60034-798-6
ISBN-10: 1-60034-798-3

www.xulonpress.com

TABLE OF CONTENTS

———— ❦ ————

ABOUT THE AUTHOR.. xi
THE CALL TO WRITE THIS BOOK........................... xix
INTRODUCTION xxiii

Chapter 1
  PUT YOUR PRAYER TO WORK FOR YOU THROUGH
  FAITH IN THE HOLY SPIRIT 29

Chapter 2
  HOW I GET JOBS THROUGH PRAYER:HOW THE
  HOLY SPIRIT WORKED FOR ME...........................37

Chapter 3
  THE FARMER'S VETERINARY "ANGEL...............49

Chapter 4
  THE MACHINE SHOP JOB 53

Chapter 5
  "OUT OF GOD'S WILL" THE WHOLESALE
  AUTOMOBILE DEALER 57

Chapter 6
    THE CABINET JOB 65

Chapter 7
    LEARNING THE CALIFORNIA
    HOUSE PRODUCTION SYSTEM..............................77

Chapter 8
    DON'T SAY SKILL-SAW..83

Chapter 9
    THE KNOTT'S BERRY FARM FOREMANS JOB...89

Chapter 10
    THE RAFTER-CUTTING JOB 95

Chapter 11
    THE ARCHITECT..99

Chapter 12
    THE VISION 103

Chapter 13
    GENE APPLEGATE..111

Chapter 14
    GOING FROM THE FIELD TO THE OFFICE........115

Chapter 15
    THE LOAN COMPANY 117

Chapter 16
    QUEENS PRIDE CABINETS DIVISION OF BETTER
    BUILDERS INC. 119

Chapter 17
  L.M. ROOFING DIVISION OF BETTER BUILDERS
  INC.(includesG.M.HARDWARE&SUPPLYDIVISION
  OF BETTER BUILDERS INC.)..............................121

Chapter 18
  MY HEART PROBLEM 128 123

Chapter 19
  THE INSURANCE COMPANY 129

Chapter 20
  THEY CAN'T FIRE YOU.......................................133

Chapter 21
  TITHING: A MUST...137

Chapter 22
  THE FIFTEEN YEAR BLIND DATE - THE LOVE
  STORY 141

Chapter 23
  LET US WALK IN THE LIGHT..............................145

REVIEWS

---⚬⚬⚬---

Your Walk with the Lord will be enhanced every day as you read this Spirit-filled book. "How to Get a Job and Keep It" is an outstanding collection of powerful, heartwarming testimonies of how the Holy Spirit has guided Gilbert through his life and how He will do the same for you. It's a book full of faith and inspiration.

Mary Goodwin
Chaplain

The candor and intimacy with which you have shared your life in this book blessed me. I know of few that have walked with the Holy Spirit as you have. In this book people can learn to walk with the Holy Spirit moment by moment. What a diverse life you have led under the direction of the Holy Spirit; some people have two or three vocations in a lifetime and I am not sure how many you had! The story of your wife Luella and how you first met on the pew of that church and later with your sister Verna Mae are beyond the realm of chance. Truly you are a man led by the Holy Spirit.

Pastor Garland B. Gauthier Jr.

When I received the manuscript of "How to Get a Job and Keep It" I leafed through the contents. At once I became interested and read several chapters. It is a hard book to put down. I believe this book will be a great asset and inspiration to anyone who will seek the Lord for His leading for all things in their walk with Him. As you read the wonderful ways the Holy Spirit has lead and supplied jobs for Gilbert every step of the way, blessed his life and increased his faith, you too will rejoice in the Lord for His care and concern for you personally.

Pastor Paul Vogler

I learned a lot by typing up this manuscript. It's encouraging to see how the Holy Spirit has worked in Gilbert's life. We all know that the Holy Spirit will never leave or forsake us. Gilbert shows us through his experiences, that the Holy Spirit wants to help us, teach us and work for us to enable us to accomplish what He has destined for our lives!

Ronna Cohen
Worship Leader/Evangelist (Jew for Jesus)
www.twohillsfountain.com

John 14:26
"But the comforter, which is the Holy Ghost, whom the Father will send in my name, He shall teach you all things, and bring all things to your remembrance, whatsoever I have said unto you."

ABOUT THE AUTHOR

I was born on a dairy and grain farm half a mile north of Springfield, Illinois. We raised chickens, hogs, dogs, cats...you name it, we had them. There were six of us children, three boys and three girls. We also raised vegetables. When I was four years old my mother would fill my red wagon with vegetables and put price tags on them. I would go down one side of the street and she would go down the other. It didn't take me long to sell my wagon out. I thought I was *big stuff*.

During the depression my folks moved from the home place to Edinberg, Illinois. It was there that Reverend Jack Gibbs had a tent meeting and later built a tabernacle with a sawdust floor. I can remember the very spot where I knelt on that sawdust at the altar and gave my heart to Jesus. I was seven or eight years old at the time.

The reason I mention Edinberg is that two miracles took place there. First, I gave my life to Jesus. Secondly, I was healed there.

At one point there was a minister visiting us for a while. His name was Roy Foster. They used to call him 'Frosty Foster.' We children called him "Uncle Roy." He was a *monster* of man and had a very deep voice. He had been a gangster and was sent to prison for selling drugs. When he went to prison, he pushed two one hundred dollar bills up his nostrils so that he could buy drugs. He was saved while in prison and had only been out a few months when he came to visit us. He could throw both of his shoulders and hips out of joint at the same time (that's when he looked like a *monster.*)

One morning my brother Glen and I had gone to the barn with our father to do our chores. Glen and I climbed up on the second story beams in the hayloft. There was a runway in the middle of the barn for the hay wagons to back in and unload hay. Log poles were lying in the runway and I fell two stories down onto the logs. I was either dead or knocked out cold. Uncle Roy came in and picked me up in his arms and prayed for me. Life came back into my body and there were no visible injuries. *Thank you Jesus!*

About this same time, after Sunday morning service I was asked to go home with the Bible family to visit for the afternoon. Brother Bible offered to let me ride their pony and gave me instructions on how *not* to ride the pony.

He told me, "You can ride him as fast as you can get him to go when you're going away from the house, but when you start back, hold him down to a gallop. If you let him run he'll jump right through the top half of the barn door."

I said to myself, *"I can handle him. I've ridden horses before."* Well, I sure was wrong this time! Coming back to the barn the pony ran as fast as he could and no matter how hard I pulled back on the reins he would not slow down. The pony ran straight for the barn door. I thought for sure he would jump straight through the top half of the door, which happened to be open. He ran up to the door as fast as he could, threw all four hooves down and abruptly stopped, trying to throw me through the upper half of the barn door, but the Holy Spirit was there watching over me. I went straight up in the air, turned a somersault and came straight down, landing on my feet with the reins still in my hands. Needless to say, I didn't get back on that pony.

If that wasn't a miracle, I don't know what is. An angel must have been riding on that pony with me.

We eventually moved back to the home place where I spent my teenage years.

At the age of nine I was required to milk one cow in the morning and one in the evening. Later on my folks started their own dairy. We milked the cows, bottled the milk and delivered it. We were the only dairy in town that went in the house and put the milk in the refrigerator, or ice box. We would knock, open the door and say "milkman" and go on in. If we carried corn roasting ears and vegetables with us it took a little longer. Now think about it. Milking cows and delivering milk was 365 days a year. **We were taught to enjoy work.** We were taught that you should have a half day's work done by 9 a.m. which was when the school bell rang. The school was two miles from our house. I can still hear my mother saying "Gilbert, you had better hurry or you're going to be late for school." I would say "No, I won't" and off I'd go in a dead run. I was never late.

My brother Glen and I started driving when we were 8 years old out on the farm. When I was 11 and Glen was 12 years of age we started delivering the milk on our own. Glen would drive while I ran the milk into the houses. I jumped off the running board and I would be half way up to the house before he got the car stopped. That's the way we were able to be on time to Sunday school at 9:30 a.m. God's angels watched over us. My mother ran the milk route most of the time. In the summer time Glen ran the milk route and I worked in the field.

Many times in the winter I was kept out of grade school to haul coal for our milk customers. I would go to the coal mine the night before so I could get my truck in line for the next morning. By the next morning there would be as many as 125 trucks waiting in line to get coal. Many times the temperature would be down below zero. I slept in a bunk house. The bunks were three bunks high all the way around the room, with a pot-belly stove in the middle of the room. It was kept red hot all the time. There were cracks as wide as your finger between the wall boards. No matter how many covers I had on, the front side of me would burn and the back side would freeze. I had to keep turning from one side to the other side all night long. I didn't get much sleep. Once in a while I could get two loads of coal in one day.

You will read in this book how the Holy Spirit has been my closest working companion down through the years. I was filled with the Holy Spirit in 1939 and He has never left my side since.

Acts 2:4
And they were all filled with the Holy Ghost, and began to speak with other tongues, as the Spirit gave them utterance."

Acts 2:17
And it shall come to pass in the last days, saith God, I will pour out of my Spirit upon all flesh: and your sons and your daughters shall prophesy, and your young men shall see visions, and your old men shall dream dreams:

God has helped me develop many talents down through the years. Here are some of them:

I have been a tumbling performer and boxing exhibitionist with W.L.S. of Chicago, IL and K.M.O.X. of St.

Louis, MO. I was also in talent shows ages 11 through 15 (together with my brother Glen). W.L.S. and K.M.O.X. had their talent shows in high school auditoriums in those days. All small towns blocked off the main street and put a stage in the middle of the street. Each Saturday night they brought in performers and a picture show. The larger towns had a stage in all of the parks. In general, Glen and I performed in most all of the towns in central Illinois. One day my mother got a phone call from the director of the Y.M.C.A. He said he had seen us boys perform. He thought we were good, but he thought he could help improve our boxing skills. There would be no charge. We went and took boxing lessons. We got to use their equipment and the swimming pool. When the Y.M.C.A. had an open house he used us to demonstrate how they could teach their boys to tumble. For doing this the Y.M.C.A. gave Glen and I life time memberships that were good anywhere in the U.S.A. We had to turn down many requests. We were in high demand, so much so that our mother felt that the performing was getting out of hand. She asked the mailman to take all of the mail that had Glen's and my name on it and keep it separate and give it to her. Unbeknownst to us, she then destroyed it. She wanted us to work for the Lord. It hurt us later when we found out, but we knew she did the right thing.

Proverbs 22:6
"Train up a child in the way he should go, and when he is old, he will not depart from it."

1. We raised grain, cattle hogs and chickens on our farm.
2. I never served an apprenticeship on any talent. The Holy Spirit started me out as a journeyman.
3. I was a machinist.
4. I was a cabinet builder.

5. I was a union carpenter.
6. I was a rafter-cutter.
7. I was a welder.
8. I was a wholesale car dealer and sold Lincoln-Mercury's.
9. I was a contractor with 5-Division Companies.
10. I was a general insurance agent.
11. I was a stock salesman with Security License.
12. I was a teacher for Dale Carnegie. ("How to Sell Without Lying to the Customer")
13. I was an incorporator with Abraham Lincoln Life Insurance Company.
14. I was an incorporator with Commonwealth Holding Company.
15. I was on the Board of Directors of Midwest Life Insurance Company of Chicago.
16. I am an architect and landscape designer.
17. God has given me a singing talent and I have written song lyrics.
18. I sang tenor with the Barber Shop Harmonizers
19. God gave me the talent to write this book.
20. We had a women's clothing company, Compatibles By Unique Products. My Daughter, Geri Lou and I manufactured the women's clothing and it was sold at house parties.
21. I built a 1934 500K Mercedes. My boy Glen and Art and Jim Nichols helped me.

I have many more talents, but **anything extraordinary that I've done has not been on my own.** I cannot take credit for any of it, especially because of my being some-what handicapped due to my limited (7th grade level) education, spelling and memorization abilities.

Henry Ford was always my inspiration. If he could build cars with a 4th grade education, **with the Holy Spirit by my side, how could I miss?**

As you come to these promises in this book, stop and re-read them and see how you can apply them to your life. God wants them to work for you too.

2 Corinthians 9:8
"God is able to make all grace abound toward you that ye always having all sufficiency in all things, may abound to every good work."

I have learned in life that it is not how much you know that counts; rather it is *what you do with what you know.*

If nothing else, this book is being written to celebrate all of the blessings that God and Jesus have bestode upon me.

THE CALL TO WRITE THIS BOOK

I never dreamed that I would ever be writing a book. There are three gifts that God did not bestow upon me: spelling, remembering names and memorization. This is why I am so overwhelmed with the things I have done in the past. I was a very poor reader. I wanted very much to read God's Word, and His promises, so I asked God to help me, and He did.

I crave reading anything that has to do with God's Word, or history. As you will see in this book God led me into working many types of jobs and professions. I remember saying some time after I left farming, though I don't remember just when, that I wanted to go into my own business. I would just work on a job long enough to learn the business, and if I didn't like that business I would quit and get a different job. That is just what I did, with the Holy Spirit's help. I never did have a problem getting a job, even in depression or recession. Other people would say they couldn't find a job. I always got the job I wanted. I couldn't understand why other people couldn't do the same thing. I figured that they just didn't want to work.

I always took it for granted that it was due to the way I was raised. We were taught to like to work. If we were caught moping around, we were punished. We were taught to do good work, always be polite and respect our elders.

One night in the latter years of my life I went to bed as usual after saying my prayers. I had asked God to help me to sleep fast. He always did, and still does. I sleep from five to seven hours at night. Around 2 a.m. I woke up **when it felt like something hit me in the head, and I could feel my brain inside my skull.**

A voice said "I want you to write a book and call it "How to Get a Job and Keep It."" I said "I can't do that." The voice said "Oh, yes you can; why do you think I have had you do all the different types of jobs that you've done? My people need your blessing conveyed to them."

I was stunned, and at that moment my mind seemed to expand and went racing back through the years. It seemed like I remembered everything that I had done since I was a child. I lay there pondering what had happened for quite some time, thinking about all the different types of jobs that I had had, and the way I had gotten them. I didn't get them in '*myself.*' Needless to say, I didn't get much sleep that night.

Mark 13:11b
"...take no thought beforehand what ye shall speak, neither do ye premeditate: but whatsoever shall be given you in that hour, that speak ye: for it is not ye that speak, BUT THE HOLY GHOST."

I suddenly realized that it was the Holy Spirit who prepared the way for me throughout my working career. He would cause me to say the right thing. He would prepare the man that interviewed me to ask the right questions, and cause Him to want to hire me. It was impossible for me (with less than a 7th grade education) to have done all the things that I had done, in *'myself'* alone. Only the Holy Spirit could have done this through me.

Isaiah 40:31
"But they that wait upon the Lord shall renew their strength, they shall mount up with wings as eagles; they shall run and not be weary, they shall walk, and not faint."

A few days later as I lay in bed after going to the bathroom I noticed a glow on the bedroom wall about half the size of a basketball. The round ball glittered as if it had sequins on it and it started moving toward the bed. As it came toward the bed the ball got larger and came around to my side of the bed. By the time the ball got to my side of the bed it was about thirty inches across, and it had a glow like a white cloud with sequins. It had a shimmering effect. The ball stayed at my side of the bed, and off the floor about three feet high. It stayed about two to three minutes and then started to move back toward the wall again. As it went toward the wall it shrunk back to half the size of a basketball and went straight through the wall, just like it came in. I didn't know what to think. Maybe this was the Holy Spirit confirming and wanting me to know that He would be with me and help me write this book. I have been stunned at how easy this as been. Thank You God and thank You, Holy Spirit.

Let us see what some of these miracles were that God's Holy Spirit has bestowed upon me.

2 Chronicles 26:5b

"As long as he sought the Lord, God made him to prosper."

Hebrews 4:16

"Let us therefore come boldly unto the throne of grace that we may obtain mercy, and find grace to help in the time of need.

INTRODUCTION

———❦———

I believe God's saints are vastly unaware of the promises and curses that are found in the Bible, and how God wants us to utilize His promises. There are over 4,000 promises (and over 400 curses) in the Bible. This book tells what the Holy Spirit and God's promises did for me, and what God wants to do for you too!

I know that the things that have taken place during my lifetime have been **unquestionably supernatural** because they cannot be explained away as merely lucky breaks. In my life, one miracle after another has taken place.

We live in the third dimension, but God wants us to move up into the fourth and fifth dimensions. He wants us to go from *glory to glory*.

2 Corinthians 3:18
"But we all, with open faces beholding as in a glass the glory of the Lord, are changed into the same image from glory to glory as by the Spirit of the Lord."

How do you do this? By reading your Bible and humbling yourself before God. Ask Him to reveal His promises to you. As for myself, as a child of God, He has given me a personal *bodyguard*, a Helper who goes ahead of me and as you will see in my writings, has come to my aid many times. You need to ask the Holy Spirit to become your *bodyguard* and be part of *your* daily life.

There is nothing hidden in God's Word that He will not reveal to your spirit, if you will humble yourself before Him, and open up your heart. Receive His promises! **The Word of God is useless as long as it stays in the pages of the Bible.** We need to transfer God's promises to our hearts and let them work for us, through God's Holy Spirit.

If you are a believer, with *all* your heart, and you open up your heart to the Scriptures and to God's promises, you will realize that there is nothing impossible with the Holy Spirit by your side. All you need to do is ask Jesus to make His promises come alive in your heart, and mind. Then act on them. The Holy Spirit will not let you down. You must not put limits on God's Holy Spirit. Have your mind and heart open to Him. Be sensitive and hear Him. He wants to bless you, but He can't do it if you are not sensitive to His voice.

Psalm 46:10a
"Be Still and know that I am God."

2 Corinthians 9:8
"God is able to make all grace abound toward you, that ye always having all sufficiency in all things, may abound to every good work."

God didn't create you to think bad things about yourself. He didn't create you to just survive and hardly make it through this wonderful world He created for us. He didn't create you for any of that nonsense. God made us to be productive and He sent the Holy Spirit, The Comforter, to help us. **Joshua 1:8-9** challenges us to believe it: **"This book of the law shall not depart out of thy mouth, but thou**

xxiv

shalt meditate therein day and night that thou mayest observe to do according to all that is written therein. For then thou shalt make thy way prosperous, and then thou shalt have good success. <u>Have I not commanded thee?</u> Be strong and of good courage, <u>be not afraid, neither be though dismayed. For the Lord thy God is with thee whithersoever thou goest.</u>"

1 Peter 2:9
"But ye are a chosen generation, a royal priest-hood, an holy nation, a peculiar people, that ye should shew forth the praises of him who hath called you out of darkness into his marvelous light."

As believers in Jesus Christ, we are set apart. We are different. We are a breed of God's own, because we have been **created by God and washed in Jesus' blood**. The Spirit of the living God dwells inside us. The same God that created the heavens and the earth **now lives in us**.

We are the temple of the Holy Ghost according to:

1 Corinthians 6:19a-20a:
"What? Know ye not that your body is the temple of the Holy Ghost which is in you. For ye are bought with a price."

We possess this treasure, this deposit of wealth in our earthen vessel. We are baptized. That means we are immersed in His power and authority. **<u>He wants His Word to operate on the inside, and outside of us.</u>** We can frame our world by the word of faith, which means we can have what we say we can have, according to His promises. We can do what we say we can, by being sensitive and letting the Holy Spirit work for us. I have tried to come at this from all angles to show how God wants you to use His promises. He also wants you to use the Holy Spirit, who is in you as a born again Christian, to accomplish your goals. ***Only Christians have this privilege***. Think about it. **Doesn't it make you want to shout?!** This is what I have done by using God's Word and letting the Holy Spirit work within me, and out of me. You can do what God says you can do, according to His promises.

Philippians 4:13
"I can do all things through Christ which strengtheneth me."

In politics, if you have the right connections you can be appointed to a high position and not have the qualifications for the job. If you are a Christian you can also start at the top of the ladder, even though you are not qualified for the job at the time, <u>in man's sight</u>. God will send the Holy Spirit and quicken your mind and teach you, so you will be well qualified for whatever job you have chosen, and you will be superior to anyone you are working with. If they try to lay you off, the Holy Spirit may not let them lay you off. If they do lay you off it will be because God has a better job for you. I will tell you about times this has happened to me, because when they find out that you are a Christian they will hate you.

John 15:18-19b
"If the world hates you, know that it hated me before it hated you, but I chose you out of the world, therefore the world hates you."

Let's look at:

Numbers 13:3a:
"Moses by the commandment of the Lord sent them from the wilderness of Paran."

God led the nation of Israel to the border of Canaan, where the people were commanded to enter the land, and take it from its inhabitants. The Bible did not say that God *suggested or instructed* them to take the Promised Land. It clearly says that He **commanded** them to take the land, to be aggressive about it, even to "Go in there and do what I, the Lord your God tells you to do!"

God is saying to you, *"Go out there and possess that job, or start that business!!"* Don't be *weak-kneed.* Go out and posses it. I will give some instructions in other chapters.

When I first started looking for jobs and I was being interviewed, I was so nervous. I shook so badly that I would grip my chair, or the desk, really tightly so the interviewer wouldn't notice me shaking. But, with the Holy Spirit nudging me, and my faith in the Holy Spirit, I would get the job. You can do it too, by using God's promises. His Holy Spirit will prepare the way for you. Your responsibility is to begin with prayer and determination.

If I can do it, I know that you can too!

Matthew 7:7-8
"Ask and it shall be given you, seek, and you shall find. Knock, and it shall be opened unto you. For everyone that asketh receiveth, and he that seeketh findeth, and to him that knocketh it shall be opened."

Chapter 1

———— ∞∞∞ ————

James 2:17
"Even so faith, if it hath not works is dead."

PUT YOUR PRAYER TO WORK FOR YOU THROUGH FAITH IN THE HOLY SPIRIT

Matthew 6:33-34a
"Seek ye first the kingdom of God, and all His righteousness, and all these things shall be added unto you. Take therefore no thought for tomorrow…"

Do not remain ignorant of God's Word and His promises. The Holy Spirit is the Helper that the Lord promised, the one who would empower His followers to be His witnesses in the world.

Right here I must interject this paragraph. It has been brought to my attention that the Holy Spirit intended for this book to be written for men only. ("Not So.")

Romans 2:11
"For there is no respect of persons with God."

This can be found several times in God's word. God's Holy Spirit will do the same for you women that He is doing for me, if you will use God's promises and the instructions in this book.

We desperately need the supernatural working of the Holy Spirit to accomplish God's purposes in our lives. There are many different ways that God wants to use us to accomplish His plan. God wants us to be witnesses through our work. **Jesus said over and over in His Word that if we would keep His commandments He would send the Holy Spirit to help us.** Spectacular miracles will take place in your life if you will apply God's Word daily.

When people get an education many forget about the Holy Spirit. You need to start thinking differently. I cannot stress the importance of this enough. **Education is power.** When you use *your* education to get a job, and leave God out of it, *who* **gets the glory?** *You do!* **You don't give glory to the miraculous power of God.**

So don't be foolish and try to do it with your own ability or education. We are not capable of doing what God wants us to do without the help of the Holy Spirit.

Praying and worshipping God with humility is the foundation and pathway to the cultivation of people who will worship God and believe His promises. Some people read God's promises, **but do not act on them**. If you will pray and worship God, it will build your faith in believing His promises.

Faith acts upon the truths of God's Word, trusting Him to provide. **Faith trusts God to reveal both the natural and supernatural to supply our needs and our healing.**

Do you have a large stone in front of you, like a grudge? Maybe someone has hurt or wronged you. **God wants you**

to forgive them and forget it, as though it was a foolish incident, because then the Holy Spirit will go to work for you. He will go before you and prepare the way when you are getting that job you want, or He'll show you the job that you should go after. He might even help you to find that love mate who He wants you to have, like the Holy Spirit did for me. ("The Blind Date Love Story") The world is missing an exciting life by not making Christ Jesus the Lord of their lives. God wants to send the Holy Spirit to help you in all of your needs, but you must empty yourself out by humbling yourself before Him and getting rid of your hang-ups.

This does not mean that you are not a Christian. It just means that you have not completely yielded your body and soul to Jesus. **The Holy Spirit wants to help us in our prayer life.**

Romans 8:26-27

"Likewise the Spirit also helpeth our infirmities, for we know not what we should pray for as we ought, but the Spirit itself maketh intercession for us with groanings which cannot be uttered. He that searcheth the hearts knoweth what is the mind of the Spirit, because He maketh intercession for the saints according to the will of God."

We have heard the expression, "Prayer changes things," but some of us ask "Why pray?" First of all prayer is a two-way communication with our Father God. His ear is tuned in to our prayers, which are a sweet smelling savor to God. Marvel not at the Holy Spirit; He is like radio and TV waves – **but much more powerful!**

John 3:18

"The wind blows wherever it pleases. You hear its sound, but you cannot tell where it comes from or

where it is going. So it is with everyone born of the Spirit."

God did not put over 4,000 promises in the pages of the Bible so you could lay it on the shelf to collect dust. God wants you to take those promises and come *boldly* <u>**to Him and ask the Holy Spirit to help you to use them.**</u>

Hebrews 4:16
"Let us therefore come *boldly* unto the throne of grace, that we may obtain mercy and grace to help in the time of need."

Ephesians 3:12
"In whom we have *boldness* unto the throne of grace, that we may obtain mercy and find grace to help in the time of need."

Prayer is the open line to heaven that connects us to the source of all power. So go ahead, be *bold*. Ask God to send the Holy Spirit to help you. I challenge you. See what the Holy Spirit will do for you.

No person can assume credit for the Holy Spirit's moving among us. But James 4:8 says "Come near to God and He will come near to you." **We draw near to God through worship, repentance, humility, desire for holiness, spiritual hunger, gratitude, submission, patience and anticipation**. Then God will draw near to you. He will then send the Holy Spirit to work for you. The Holy Spirit will help you in deciding what job you should look for. The Holy Spirit will go before you and prepare the way, just like He has done for me.

Proverbs 30:5
"Every word of God is pure. He is a *shield* unto them that put their trust in Him."

Psalm 32:8
"I will instruct thee and teach thee in the way
which thou shalt go. I will guide thee with Mine eye."

Zechariah 4:6b
"'Not by might, nor by power, but by My Spirit,'
saith the Lord of Hosts."

God gives us talents, but we must let the Holy Spirit help
us develop them. Don't try to develop them by yourself. Oh
yes, one more thing, God has no use for laziness and we
must give God at least 10% of our income. That's all He asks
for in return for what He is doing for us.

AVOID PRAYER FORMS

The great evangelist Charles G. Finney states, "We see
from this subject the absurdity of using set forms of prayer,
or prayer books. The very idea of using a form rejects the
leading of the Holy Spirit. Nothing is more calculated to
destroy the Spirit of prayer, and entirely darken and confuse
the mind to what constitutes prayer, than prayer forms. Prayer
forms are not only absurd in themselves, but they are the very
device of the devil to destroy the spirit and break the power
of prayer. It does not matter if the form is a good one. Prayer
does not consist of written words. It does not matter what
the words are if the heart is not led by the Spirit of God. If
the desire is not kindled, the thoughts directed and the whole
current of feeling produced and led by the Spirit of God **it is
not PRAYER**." Set forms keep an individual from praying
from the heart. **Your prayers must come from your heart.**

Hebrews 6:12
"That ye be not slothful, but followers of them who
through faith and patience inherit the promises."

The promises that Abraham obtained are the same promises that we Christians are presently inheriting, healing and prosperity.

Galatians 3:29 (T.L.B.)
"And now that we are Christ's we are the true descendants of Abraham and all of God's promises to him belong to us."

Why is it that Christians do not grab hold of these promises and use them? All you have to do is ask and seek, and the Holy Spirit will be there to help you. I just quoted Hebrews 6:12 (**"BE NOT SLOTHFUL."**) Sometimes I think most Christians are ___big babies___.

Genesis 12:3
I will bless them that bless thee, and curse him that curseth thee. And in thee shall all families of the earth be blessed."

It is hard to stop quoting promises, because there are so many. God wants me to whet your appetite. I could fill my book with them. But God's Holy Spirit wants you to seek them out for yourself and apply them to your need. You must renew your mind. <u>**Until your mind has been renewed to total belief in God's Word it will be hard for you to grasp what God wants you to absorb out of this book.**</u> We must have our minds renewed to the truth of material prosperity, as God has promised us in the Abrahamic Covenant.

I told a Minister some of the things that God's Holy Spirit had done for me. I thought he would be thankful for what God's Holy Spirit had done. But he said I was a flat out liar. He needed his mind renewed. I felt sorry for him. He was the same age that I was. He has been dead for nine years (as of this writing.) In his last years he suffered untold agony. Do not make light of the Holy Spirit's workings!

UNBELIEF

Unbelief is the major stronghold in every person – saved or lost. In a Christian it is designed to keep him from really believing certain truths in God's Word that will make him powerful and effective in God's Kingdom. He will then be able to do things that he never dreamed were possible.

God has provided powerful tools for us to use as Christians in seeking a job, or going into a business. There is nothing more powerful than God's promises through His Holy Spirit. **His promises are more powerful than the atom bomb**. So, let's get familiar with these powerful promises. God will cause them to come alive by our humbling ourselves on our knees and pouring our hearts out to Him.

Jeremiah 29:13
'Ye shall seek me, and find me when ye shall search for me with all your heart."

Chapter 2

Philippians 4:13
"I can do all things through Christ which strength-
eneth me."

HOW I GET JOBS THROUGH PRAYER: HOW THE HOLY SPIRIT WORKED FOR ME

He wants to work for you too, but the average person holds the Holy Spirit away at an arms length. It seems that people are afraid of Him and feel that their education will do it for them. Or, <u>they feel unworthy, too embarrassed or just too "proud" to ask God to send the Holy Spirit to help them in their daily activities,</u> and in time of need. Maybe you feel you just don't need God. With His help we can invade the impossible; when it seems that there is no other way, the Holy Spirit will make a way.

    "STOP". Before you read any further, are you a half hearted Christian that warms the church pews? If you are, then you need to rededicate your life to Jesus. This book will not help you if you read it like a story, or literature. You must apply what you are reading to your heart, and mind. If you are not a born again Christian then apply these scriptures to your heart, so you will be ready for heaven.

Romans 3:10-23

As it is written, There is none righteous, no, not one: There is none that understandeth, there is none that seeketh after God. They are all gone out of the way, they are together become unprofitable; there is none that doeth good, no, not one. Their throat is an open sepulchre; with their tongues they have used deceit; the poison of asps is under their lips: Whose mouth is full of cursing and bitterness: Their feet are swift to shed blood: Destruction and misery are in their ways: And the way of peace have they not known: There is no fear of God before their eyes. Now we know that what things soever the law saith, it saith to them who are under the law: that every mouth may be stopped, and all the world may become guilty before God. Therefore by the deeds of the law there shall no flesh be justified in his sight: for by the law is the knowledge of sin. But now the righteousness of God without the law is manifested, being witnessed by the law and the prophets; Even the righteousness of God which is by faith of Jesus Christ unto all and upon all them that believe: for there is no difference: For all have sinned, and come short of the glory of God;

1. Admit you are a sinner. "There is no one righteous, not even one — for all have sinned and fall short of the glory of God."
2. Romans 10:13 Everyone who calls upon the name of the Lord will be saved.
3. Romans 10:9 If you confess with your mouth, "Jesus is Lord" and believe in your heart that God raised him from the dead, **you will be saved**.

If you applied these scriptures to your heart and mind, you are now ready to continue reading this book, and it will come alive in you.

Philippians 2:5
"Let this mind be in you which was also in Christ Jesus."

How do we put Christ's mind in us? By putting God's Word in us by reading the Bible, and humbling ourselves on our knees in prayer. This is what people refuse to do. If we let the Holy Spirit work for us we will not make all of those foolish mistakes. God wants us to grab hold of His promises and use them. God put over 4,000 promises in the Bible and He expects us to use them – or else He would not have given them to us. This is why so many Christians do not prosper. They are just plain *lazy.*

Proverbs 13:4
"The soul of the lazy people want much but get little, while the diligent are prospering."

There is a type of man whose form should be cast in timeless bronze and his statue placed in every college of the land. It's not "book learning" that young men need. Nor do they need instructions about this and that. What the model man needs is a stiffening of the vertebrae which will cause him to be loyal, trustworthy and to act promptly, concentrating his energies to do the right thing.

Slipshod assistance, foolish inattention, shabby indifference and half-hearted work seem to be the rule of the day. No man succeeds unless by *hook or crook,* or threat or bribe. Some men are lucky enough to get God's help without their even asking, but this is not the man whom God will bless.

Because of our lazy indifferences this is what God will have His Holy Spirit do to us. What we have will be given to others!

Luke 19:24
"He said unto them that stood by, 'Take him the pound, and give it to him that hath ten pounds.'"

A young lady asked me what she should say when she is being interviewed for a job. I told her to tell the interviewer, "I am a person who likes to work, and I will strive to be the best employee you have ever had. I will make you money."
She said "Make him money! I want to make the money!" I said, "Then don't apply for the job."
She said, "Why?" I said, "If you don't intend to make your employer money he can't pay you."
She said, "Oh, I see what you mean."
If you are a true dedicated Christian and you have prayed about your job, **the Holy Spirit will guide you in what to say, and He will teach you on the job.** You will find in other chapters how the Holy Spirit has worked for me. You cannot be successful as a Christian without prayer. Like I said in the last chapter, prayer is the open line to heaven that connects us to the source of all power.

Hebrews 4:16
"Let us therefore come *boldly* unto the throne of grace, that we may obtain mercy and grace to help in the time of need."

Ephesians 3:12 (R.S.V.)
"In whom we have boldness, confidence of access through our faith in Him and access with confidence by the faith of Him."

Luke 12:12
**"For the Holy Ghost shall teach you
in the same hour what ye ought to say."**

As you read this book you will see how the Holy Spirit showed me what to say. He taught me on the job how to do jobs that I had never done.

Exodus 4:15
"And thou shalt speak unto him, and put words in his mouth; and I will be with thy mouth, and with his mouth, and will teach you what ye shall do."

Philippians 4:13
"I can do all things through Christ which strengtheneth me."

I cannot stress these verses enough! I stand on these and so should you!

There are over 4000 promises in the Bible and it seems that very few people know that they are there. If they do know that they're in the Bible they seem to ignore them. The people have enough education that they don't think they need God's help. God's Word says that in the last days the people will be ever learning but never coming to the knowledge of the truth.

Romans 1:22
"Professing themselves to be wise, they became fools."

When you are faithful in your prayer life and absorbing God's Word, God will honor you and bless you and your family. As the song goes, *'I am learning to lean on Jesus, gaining more power than I ever dreamed. I'm learning to lean on Jesus.'*

Isaiah 40:31
"But they that wait upon the Lord shall renew their strength, they shall mount up with wings as eagles; they shall run and not be weary; and they shall walk, and not faint."

I remember when I would be driving to get a job, or going out to look for a job. Many times I would be praying and worshiping the Lord, and praying in the heavenly language. I would feel like I was floating through the air. I would be thanking God for the job that He was going to give me, thanking Him for the job that He had already given me – and the Holy Spirit never did let me down.

When you go to get a job, always find out what kind of a position they want to fill. Find out something about that job, even if you have to go to the library and get a book, and read up on it. When you are being interviewed orally tell the interviewer this, or write it on the application, or attach a separate piece of paper to the application. You say, or write this:

1. Mr. X, I am a person who likes to work. I just enjoy working.
2. You need me; I will make you money. (If he is interviewing you orally, say nothing until he answers you; "The first one that speaks loses!" When you ask a question, do not (DO NOT) say anything until the other person speaks.) He might say, "I don't need you right now; maybe later on." You say, **"Yes you do need me. He will say, "Why do I need you?" "Because I will make you money. Mr. X, you need me. I like to work and I will take an interest in**

<u>your company</u>." If he again says, "No, I don't need you" you say, "<u>**You didn't hear me did you? I said I will make you money.**</u>" I will guarantee you that he will reply, "Maybe I do need you," and he or she will hire you.

When you get the job make sure that you do these things:

1. <u>**Never talk to other employees during working hours, only if it's a question about your work, and then make it brief and get back to work.**</u>
2. <u>**When you walk from one place to another walk quickly. Don't be a slouch and mope when you walk from one place to another.**</u>
3. <u>**Always work a little faster than your co-workers. If your co-workers tell you to slow down say, "OK." Slow down for a little while then gradually speed back up. When you are working on a job you should work for your employer as through the business was your own.**</u> For the Lord God says in:

Ephesians 5:6-7
"Don't work hard only when your master is watching and then shirk when he isn't looking; work hard and with gladness all the time, as though working for Christ, doing the work of God with all your hearts. Remember, the Lord will pay you for each good you do, whether you are slave or free."

4. <u>**Always be a little bit early to work. Don't take advantage of your privileges. If someone asks you a question you don't know the answer to say "Why**</u>

did you ask me that question?" He will answer his own question. TRUST ME. It works.

God didn't create you to be skittish and think bad things about yourself. He didn't create you to survive and just hardly make it through life. He didn't create you for any of that nonsense. God made you to be productive. This is **what Joshua 1:8-9 says:**

Joshua 1:8-9
"This book of the law shall not depart out of thy mouth, but thou shalt meditate therein day and night that thou mayest observe to do according to all that is written therein. For then thou shalt make thy way prosperous, and then thou shalt have good success. Have I not commanded thee? Be strong and of good courage, be not afraid, neither be though dismayed. For the Lord thy God is with thee whithersoever thou goest."

The Bible says that we are a peculiar generation.

1 Peter 2:9
"Ye are a chosen generation, a royal priesthood, an holy nation, a peculiar people, that ye should shew forth the praises of Him who hath called you out of darkness into His marvelous light."

We are set apart. We are different. We are a breed of our own because we **have been created by Christ and washed in His blood.** The Spirit of the Living God dwells inside of us. **The same God that created the heavens and the earth now lives in us.** We are the temple of the Holy Ghost according to:

1 Corinthians 6:19-20:
"What? Know ye not that your body is the temple
of the Holy Ghost which is in you, which ye have of
God, and ye are not your own? For ye are bought with
a price. Therefore glorify God in your body, and in
your spirit, which are God's."

The Bible says we are to possess this treasure, this deposit of wealth in earthen vessels. We are baptized. That means we are immersed in His power and authority. He wants His Word to operate on the inside of us. We can frame our world by the Word of God and faith. We can have what we say we can have. We can do what we say we can do. This is what I have done by using God's promises through faith. We can be what God says we can be according to:

Isaiah 55:11
"So shall My Word be that goeth forth out of My
mouth. It shall not return unto Me void, but it shall
accomplish that which I please, and it shall prosper in
the thing whereto I sent it."

We don't owe the world anything. The world should be glad we are here.

In politics, if you have the right connections you can be appointed to a high position and not have the qualifications for the job. You don't have to start at the bottom of the ladder.

If you are a Christian you can start at the top of the ladder, even though you are not qualified for the job in man's sight. God will send the Holy Spirit and quicken your mind and teach you, so you will be well qualified for whatever job you have chosen, and be superior to anyone you are working with. If they try to lay you off, the Holy Spirit may not let them. If you are laid off God has a better job for you.

I experienced this on two different occasions. The foreman tried to lay me off and the superintendent would not let him do it. I knew that the Holy Spirit was working on my behalf.

Hebrews 4:12

For the word of God is quick, and powerful, and sharper than any two edged sword, piercing even to the dividing asunder of soul and spirit, and of the joints and marrow, and is a discerner of the thoughts and intents of the heart.

In 1952 we moved to Brea, California and I was in need of a job. When I got out of bed I knelt by my bed and prayed like this:

I thank You for the companionship and good relationship I have with my wife. I thank You Lord for my health. I thank You for the rest You gave me last night and I thank You for healthy children.

After about ten minutes of praying like this I prayed for some missionaries, pastors, our President, our armed forces and salvation for the lost. The Bible says to pray for those in authority over us. I then got *BOLD* and talked to God like this: (I talk to God just like I would talk to my earthly father when he made promises to me):

Father God, You gave me a wonderful family. It is my obligation to supply their needs. Your Word says in 1 Timothy 5:8 "But if any provide not for his own and especially for those of his own house, __he hath denied the faith, and is worse than an infidel__."

After I prayed for fifteen minutes I read the Bible, but first I asked Jesus to sit down with me and reveal His Word to me as though He were here with me **(that's when the Bible comes alive.)**

After I have read the Bible I talk to Jesus and the Holy Spirit one more time. You have said in Your Word that You will send Your Holy Spirit to help me if I ask You. Well, I am asking You now. God, you know that I am not experienced in many skills. I am expecting You to teach me just like Your Word says You will do. I know that You have given me talents, but I need You to help me develop them.

For whom the LORD loveth he correcteth; even as a father the son in whom he delighteth.

Luke 12:12

"For the Holy Ghost shall teach you in the same hour what ye ought to say."

Help me Father to be the best man that my employer has ever hired. Now Lord I am going to the carpenter's union hall (or to look for work) and I know that there will be other men wanting jobs also, but I expect Your Holy Spirit to keep a job for me. I thank You Father for the job You have for me. I thank You Father for the job You are going to give me and I pray this in the name of Jesus. Amen.

It is very important to thank God for your job before you get it. If nothing else it is just good manners.

In Number 13 God has led the children of Israel to the border of Canaan where the people were commanded to enter the land and take it from its inhabitants. God did not just suggest that they take the promised land. The Bible doesn't say He instructed them to take it. It clearly says **He commanded them to take it,** to be aggressive about it, even. "Go in there and do what I, the Lord your God, tells you to do!"

GO OUT THERE AND POSSESS THAT JOB. YOU MUST EXERCISE YOUR FAITH SO IT WILL WORK FOR YOU.

God's Holy Spirit will quicken those dead cells in your brain and you will be astounded at what He will do for you.

Romans 4:17-b
"God, who quickeneth the dead and calleth those things which be not as though they were.

If you get a job by using the instructions in this book and then go on the job and mope around and goof up, *so help you God*! The Holy Spirit will punish you.

Proverbs 3:12
For whom the LORD loveth he correcteth; even as a father the son in whom he delighteth.

Chapter 3

---⸎⸎⸎---

Philippians 4:17
"My God shall supply all your needs according to
His riches in glory by Christ Jesus."

THE FARMER'S
VETERINARY "ANGEL"

In 1942 I was on a 105 acre farm raising 12 feeder cattle, 100 head of hogs per year, corn, soy beans and alfalfa for hay. I raised and fed the cattle until they weighed 750 pounds or more. I fed the hogs so that they would weigh between 125 and 150 pounds, before I took them to the stockyards to be sold.

One morning I went to the barn to do my feeding and found one of my fattest hogs had turned blue. I had never seen anything like that before. I ran to the house and called the first veterinarian that I found in the phone book. I told him about the hog being blue and he said my hog had "*the cholera.*"

"*Cholera!*" I said, "Man, what will I do?" The veterinarian said that my hogs needed to be vaccinated. I said *"Hurry and get out here and vaccinate them!"* "No," he said, "You come to my office and I will teach you how to vaccinate your own hogs – then you can do it yourself."

When I hung up the phone I just stood there scratching my head. I couldn't figure out why he didn't want to come out and vaccinate the hogs himself, so he could make around $100. I was stumped. But I had no time to lose, so I jumped in my car and *beat* it into the veterinarian's office as fast as I could.

I was surprised to find out that this veterinarian hospital was just a '*hole-in-the-wall*,' so to speak. He showed me how many "cc's" to vaccinate each hog with, and how to vaccinate the hog in the armpit. He sold me the syringe and vaccine that I would need.

"I have something else for you," he told me, "if you will promise never to tell anyone who gave it to you." "I promise I will never tell anyone." I said. I had no idea what he was about to give me. He then said, "I have feeding formulas for you to use when you feed your cattle and your hogs. This feeding formula will cause your cattle and your hogs to gain weight faster than the feed that you are buying at "the Elevator."

I again told him "I will never tell anyone who gave me the formula." (And I never did tell anyone who gave me that formula – except, I believe he was an *angel!*

Hebrews 13:2
"Be not forgetful to entertain strangers, for thereby some have entertained angels unaware.

I went back to the farm and vaccinated my hogs like the *veterinarian* had told me to do. He told me to kill the blue hog and call the rendering works to come and pick him up, which I did.

I had been buying cattle and hog feed from the Bradforton Elevator. When I changed over to the veterinarian's formula for my cattle and hogs, the Elevator man asked why I was not going to use his formula anymore. I said that I wanted to mix my own feed. The Elevator man laughed at me. He said that his feed was just as good as what I was mixing.

I noticed right away that the cattle and hogs were filling out better. I had a farm scale in the barn lot, so I weighed some of the cattle separately and found that they were gaining an average of three pounds every day. I had bought scrub cattle (the scrubs were the ones that no one else wanted.) Purebred cattle are not known to put on more than three pounds per day.

My hogs were ready for market two to three weeks sooner than animals that were on the Elevator hog feed. When I took my hogs to the stockyards I got top price for them. The other farmers would come around my hog pen and ask how I got my hogs to look like that. One 50 year old man said he had been raising hogs all his life and he had never been able to get his hogs to look like mine.

"How do you do it?" he asked. I just stood there and didn't say anything.

I remember one load of cattle that I took to St. Louis Stockyards. I got top price for them too. radio station K.M.O.X. always showcased cattle and hogs that topped the market that day. My load of cattle made the news that day.

I kept the feed formula that the *veterinarian* had written on two pieces of scrap paper in a little oak receipt box that my mother had given me. Every now and then I would get the box out of the safe and re-read the formulas.

One day in 1998 I opened the safe and looked in the little oak box and the formulas were **gone!** I asked my wife Luella if she knew where they were. I also asked my children if they had seen them. They all were as stunned as I was. God gave those formulas to me and God took them away, I guess! What else could have happened to them? **I truly believe that this "good looking" *veterinarian* was one of**

51

God's angels. GOD'S HOLY SPIRIT WANTS TO DO THE SAME FOR YOU.

Acts 27:23
"For there stood by me this night the angel of God, whose I am, and whom I serve."

Chapter 4

———— ⦿ ————

Philippians 4:13
"I can do all things through Christ Jesus which strengtheneth me."

THE MACHINE SHOP JOB

In this book I will be quoting some scriptures more than once because they are very powerful scriptures to use when you want the Holy Spirit to help you.

In January of 1945 we moved to Pasadena California. My brother Glen was working as a machinist for Odekirk & Ludwig Machine Shop in Pasadena. While I was still on the farm I wanted to prepare for a rainy day. The Government had a Machine training program in Springfield, Illinois, where I was farming. So, during one winter I went one night a week to the school. I made two little shop hammer heads on the lathe and that was all I made. The school gave me a little booklet that had pictures of different types of lathes, mills, drill presses, and so forth. My brother Glen said "why don't you come and put in your application where I work." So I did, but I prayed and said "Lord I know very little about running machine tools. The Lord said "take that little book that the government school gave you and write on the application the names of some of the lathes and mills, and so forth." So I did. God said "Don't I say in my Word in:

Exodus 4:15
And thou shalt speak unto him, and put words in his mouth and I will be with thy mouth and with his mouth, and will TEACH YOU WHAT YE SHALL DO.

And, in:

Luke 12:12
FOR THE HOLY GHOST SHALL TEACH YOU IN THE SAME HOUR WHAT YE OUGHT TO SAY."

I said "Yes, Lord. I will believe and trust you."

Prayer is the open line to heaven that connects us to the source of all POWER.

So, I filled out the application and they hired me, no questions asked. As I went to work the next day and the foreman put me on a lathe, I was lathing rocket shells. I had to cut them to a very small tolerance. With the Holy Spirit on my side how could I do anything wrong? I don't remember spoiling one rocket tube. I started as a journeyman machinist, not an apprentice. After I was there a few weeks, myself, my brother Glen and three or four more men were asked if we would come to work at 4:00 a.m. in the morning and work until 7:00 a.m., stopping to eat our breakfast, then go back to work at 8:00 a.m. with the other men. That went on for a few weeks until some of the other men started to complain. We then had to stop. The men that complained were considered to be "deadheads." I worked there until August of 1945. The war was still going on out in the West Pacific Islands. One day while we were working someone came running into our shop yelling. "THE WAR IS OVER...THE WAR IS OVER." We all knew what that meant. But we didn't know how soon it would happen.

We continued to work that day and about 2:00 p.m. all kinds of airplanes came flying overhead. They were flying very low to the ground. There were B29s, B17 Bombers, P51s, P38s and many more different kinds of airplanes. It looked as if there was a 100 or more of them. The war was over, so that evening it happened. They laid everyone off. When that happened I simply asked God to direct me to another job.

Mark 11:24
"Therefore I say unto you, what things so ever ye desire when ye pray, believe that ye receive them and ye shall have them."

Chapter 5

Jeremiah 10:2
"Thus saith the Lord, learn not the way of the heathen, and be not dismayed at the signs of heaven, for the heathen are dismayed at them."

"OUT OF GOD'S WILL" THE WHOLESALE AUTOMOBILE DEALER

I am putting this in this book to show how easy it is to get out of God's will. As you will see, God did not want me in the automobile wholesale business, or retail car sales.

After WWII I bought a few cars from private parties and resold them. I made good money on the cars. We had moved to Decatur, Illinois, where Luella's folks lived, and where her father was a real estate broker. He sold us a small house that needed remodeling for $3,500.

Decatur at that time had two automobile auctions. The two auto auctions were considered to be the world's largest. Dealers would come from as far away as California to buy cars at these two auctions. My father-in-law suggested that he and I get our car dealer licenses. He said that he had a friend who was a dealer, who would teach me the trade. He was a wholesale dealer himself. He and other dealers would go to Cleveland Ohio and other towns in the east, and buy cars from other car dealers. My father-in-law said he would loan me the money and help me clean the cars up, and polish them. We would then sell the cars on the auction and split the profit. That sounded really good to me. He introduced me to his friend, Bill. Bill said that I could go with him on his next trip that weekend. We would always go east on Sunday evening. (Right off, this was not good. I had to miss going to church on Sunday evening with my family.)

We went on the train to Chicago, then we transferred to another train that took us onto Cleveland, Ohio. We road the night train most of the night. Other dealers would go along also. Bill was the nicest man you would ever want to meet, and he was an honest car dealer. He didn't smoke or drink and I don't recall hearing him swear. But he did have one weakness, "WOMANIZING."

He showed me how to approach the car dealers and how to bid on the cars. I caught on real quickly. We would buy two cars each and then tow-bar one car behind the lead car. We would get into Decatur on Wednesday or Thursday, and it was then time for my father-in-law to help me clean and polish the cars. If there were any dents in the cars Bill used a body shop out in the country that would repair them for a reasonable price.

My father-in-law and I started to clean and polish the cars. We had gotten the first car about half cleaned and polished when my partner (father-in-law) said he was so beat that he couldn't help me finish the job. I had to finish cleaning and polishing the two cars by myself. I had the car ready for the Thursday auto auction. I don't remember how much I made on the cars, but I do remember that I was very happy with the amount. I took the check to my father-in-law so we could settle up. I thought that since he had only worked on part of the first car that he would compensate me for that. But he didn't. He took half of the profit and he continued to do that on future car deals. At that time I had no place else that I could borrow money. So I was stuck with my father in law.

Later on I said something about it and he said he would charge me a percentage instead. He charged me 25% which was usury and against the law. You could not go above 10%. I was young and I had a wife and child to feed, so I paid him. I lost money on my cars one week. Guess what? He still charged me the 25%. I told one of the car dealers in Cleveland, Ohio what my father-in-law was charging me. He said, "That's illegal. What's the matter with that guy?" This car dealer said he would loan me all the money I needed at 6%. When I told my father-in-law what the automobile dealer was going to do for me, he just sat there and stared at me with his mouth hanging open. At that time it was illegal to charge more than 10% and anything over that was usury. That made it illegal. Luella and I were hurt, but the bible says to forgive those that hurt you, and that is what we did.

1 John 3:15
"Whosoever hateth his brother is a murderer: and ye know that no murderer hath eternal life abiding in him."

Proverbs 10:12
"Hatred stirreth up strifes: but love covereth all sins."

I continued going east, buying cars. My young brother Guy came to Decatur and lived with Luella and I for a while. He drove cars for me while he was there. One time we were driving on ice and he slid in the ditch. We were fortunate that the cars were not damaged. Another time I was tow-baring a car at 70 miles per hour. (Dry, wet, or on black ice – this was the speed I always drove.) I ran into solid ice with ruts in it.

The cars slid sideways down the road. By the time I got the cars slowed down the lead car went down an embankment. The tow-bar car was sitting on the highway and it was after dark. I ran back to the tow car, jumped into it and started the engine up. I pulled both cars across the highway. I could see head lights beaming down the road toward me. Just as I got the cars over the center line of the road a Greyhound bus came flying by at about 70 miles per hour. God's Holy Spirit was protecting me and watching over me. (He will do the same for you if you will humble yourself, and yield to Him.)

One time I bought a taxi from a company that was going broke. It was on a Saturday evening and the loan company that he had the loan on the car with was closed. He promised me that he would take my check to the loan company on Monday morning, pay the car off and send me the title. But he didn't. (HE LIED!) He spent my money for something else. I was fortunate. Even though I did not know it, the Holy Spirit was watching over me.

My dealer friend Bill knew how to get a title and license for the car. He had me get what is known as a Sheriff's Title. I then sold the car on the auction and made about $500. I was sure afraid for awhile. I soon decided that the whole-sale automobile business was not for me. I feel that the Holy Spirit made me feel very uncomfortable in that type of business even though I was making good money. For one thing, I had to be away from my family most of the week. I had never done that, and have always refused to take a job that kept me away from my family. But the number two reason was that as soon as we got to Cleveland they hunted for women to be with, and sleep with. They were continually urging me to do the same. One of the dealers had a garage business with a house trailer parked in it. He let Guy and I sleep in it. That saved us from paying a hotel bill. He would always ask us if we would like for him to send us a couple of girls to sleep with us. Of course we would say, "No thank you."

This was the year 1947 and WWII had only been over about 2 years. The automobile factories were just gearing up their production and the bottom fell out in one week. For my part, I was glad. It gave me an excuse to get out of the whole-sale car business. At that time my father-in-law wanted to buy a new Chevrolet. Everyone wanted to buy a new car right after WWII. He asked me if I could get him one and I said, "Yes I could, for $2,500." He had been looking around and gotten some prices. He said my price was way too high. He said a dealer had a whole clover field of new cars down at Edwardsville, Illinois. That was about 125 miles southwest of Decatur. He said that he could get a new Impala Chevrolet for $1,800, but he would have to pay for it in advance and wait in line. I said there had to be something wrong. It was impossible to buy a new car at that price. People were paying from $500 to $1,000 over list price for new cars. I was right. It was a scam. The car dealer ran to Arizona, but the Feds caught up with him and sent him to prison.

My father-in-law never did get his money back. God took the money that he had taken from me.

Remember the car body shop men that had a body shop out in the country, that did my car body work? I always thought that there was something not right out there. After I went out of the car business and was working on the Stally Elevator job, the FBI came on the job and arrested the two brothers. I was told by Bill that the FBI investigated me because I had cars repaired at their body shop. I always felt that there was something strange taking place at their shop. They had a room in the back of the shop that they always kept locked. When one of the brothers would go into that room he would unlock the door, go in and lock the door behind him. When he came out he would lock the door again. The rumor was that they had a short wave set in the room. I never did find out for sure what they had in that room. I did find out what they were arrested for though. They would get a late model wrecked car that had a good engine in it. They would then go out and steal a car with the same body style and they would switch the serial number name plate on the door post, and switch the engine. They would have a driver drive the car to Texas and sell it on the auction.

Proverbs 7:27
Her house is the way to hell, going down to the chambers of death.

Proverbs 15:24
The way of life is above to the wise, that he may depart from hell beneath.

Later on I was asked if I would like to sell cars for the Lincoln Mercury new car dealer in Decatur. He said he would send me to the Ford sales school in St. Louis. I said OK and I went to the school. For something like this I always took my tape recorder and taped the teaching so I could later review it. Am I glad I taped what that teacher was teaching. Boy am I glad! The whole week of teaching was nothing but a bunch of lies on how to sell cars by lying to the customers. I could not believe what these men were being put through. He swore like a drunken sailor also. After a couple of days he noticed me taping the teaching session. He approached me with his face as red as a beet. He asked me what I was going to do with the tapes. I told him I used them to rehearse the sales pitches. I sold cars for a few weeks, but that ended my career as a car salesman. I was so disgusted with that sales school.

Paul Malachi 2:6
"The law of truth was in his mouth, and iniquity was not found in his lips: he walked with me in peace and equity, and did turn many away from iniquity."

Psalms 119:72
"The law of thy mouth is better unto me than thousands of gold and silver."

I later taught for Dale Carnegie. We had salesmen from all different companies come to our school wanting to know how to sell without lying to their customers about their product. I was shocked, but that was what we taught. We taught them how to sell their product without lying. I had a lot of fun doing it. I have sold a lot of different products and I have never lied to sell any of them. Sometimes people hear what they want to hear, but not what was really being said. My mother used to say "If you can't tell the truth, don't say anything." If someone asks you a question and you don't know the answer, always, and I repeat, always ask, "Why do you ask that question?" They will always answer their own question. Don't try to answer it. Tell them you will find out the answer and get it back to them. They will always respect you for your honesty.

Chapter 6

Ephesians 3:12 (R.S.V.)
**"In whom we have boldness and confidence of
access through our faith in Him."**

THE CABINET JOB
(25 cents over union scale)

We were living in Decatur, Illinois in 1949. I had just gotten out of the Wholesale Automobile business. I needed a job. I prayed and asked God what kind of a job I should look for. I wanted a job that I could learn a trade so I could go into my own business. If I became a plumber I would always be a subcontractor, the same with an electrician. I did not want to be a subcontractor. I was looking through the paper in the want-ads and **I asked God what I should look for.** (At this point I want you to pay close attention to this chapter in this book. As my life unfolds throughout the book you'll see how the Holy Spirit has done some phenomenal things.)

My eyes fastened onto a cabinet making job at Walarus Manufacturing Company. I asked God "should I apply for that job?" I felt strongly that I should. Yes, that would be a good place to start to learn to be a general contractor. There was just one catch. I had never built a cabinet! Here is where my belief in God's promises was going to be tested.

Luke 12:12
"For the Holy Ghost shall teach you in the same hour what ye ought to say."

I went down and applied for the job. Mr. Gray Jr., the son of the owner interviewed me. The first question he asked me was "can you build cabinets?" I said, "Yes."

Philippians 4:13
"I can do all things through Christ which strengtheneth me.

When I testify to people at gatherings I ask them if they think I lied to Mr. Gray. Most say "Yes." I ask you, "What do you think?" I say, "if I lied then the Bible is a lie." What does that scripture say? It doesn't say "some things." It says **"all things."** It doesn't say that you need to know anything about the job you have applied for. If you believe in the Bible at all, then you have to believe these scriptures.

Exodus 4:15
And thou shalt speak unto him, and put words in his mouth: and I will be with thy mouth, and with his mouth, <u>and will teach you what ye shall do.</u>

I asked him if there were any special tools that I would need. He said "No, just the usual hand tools." After a little bit of chit-chat He said "OK, I will hire you." He said their company was a union shop and I had 30 days to join the union. When I applied for the job I didn't know that the company was a union shop. When you are inexperienced and you join a union you are required to begin as an apprentice. An apprentice starts at a very low wage. He must train for four years with a journeyman. Then he can earn journeyman wages. I had never built a cabinet. I didn't even have any tools. I had to go to a "hock-shop" to buy my tools. I asked when I should come to work. Mr. Gray said I could start Monday. I started to get up like I was going to leave. Then I asked, "By the way, what does this job pay?" He told me the union scale. I said fine, shook his hand and started to leave again. (A voice spoke to me and said "Ask him for 25 cents over scale!") For some reason I didn't hesitate. I said, "If I can do the job that I have said that I can do, then I want 25 cents over scale on my fourth pay check, or that will be my last week here." Mr. Gray reared back in his chair and thought for a little bit and then said "Alright, I will do it." (Right here there is one thing I want to caution you. When you ask a question like I did, you must not say another word, even if it seems like two or three minutes go by. The first one that speaks loses. This is a rule you never want to forget.) I could not figure out what caused me to ask for that extra 25 cents per hour. It had to be the Holy Spirit speaking through me. I would not have done that in myself.

As I said, I didn't have any carpenter tools, so I went to some hock shops and bought used tools. I went home and sharpened and polished the tools. On Monday morning I clocked in and they introduced me to the foreman. He assigned a work bench to me. He then handed me a set of blue prints that had three sheets to them. The foreman said that if I needed any help to come to him and he would help me.

Thank You Holy Spirit! I spread out the blue prints and looked at them. To my amazement the blue prints looked like I had already memorized them and I was used to reading blueprints. Thank You Lord!

If you will remember, I prayed and asked God to show me the job I should have. I also expected the Holy Spirit to show me how, and teach me on the job. He did this, just like God's Word says.

James 1:5-6
If any of you lack wisdom, let him ask of God, that giveth to all men liberally, and unbraideth not; and it shall be given him. But let him ask in faith, nothing wavering. For he that wavereth is like a wave of the sea driven with the wind and tossed.

Because of my unwavering faith and steadfast belief in God's Word, the Holy Spirit was working for me, and in me. He was expanding my mind. Every time I realize this is happening I thrill from head to toe. I can sing. I am thrilled to walk with Jesus day by day. Before the day went by I was introduced to the union steward. Like a fool I told him that I was to get 25 cents an hour over union scale on my fourth pay check. He said, "You will never get it." I asked why. He said, "Because we are trying to get a 5 cents per hour raise and we can't get that. If we can't get 5 cents how do you think you're going to get 25 cents per hour over scale?" He scoffed at me. I said "Then I will not be here after my fourth pay check." (My faith did not waiver.)

We were allotted a certain amount of time to build a cabinet, desk or chair. I had no problem meeting the time schedule. Everything seemed to be going smoothly. I was sworn into the union and the forth week was coming up. I had not seen Mr. Gray since he hired me. It was now Tuesday, the day that the time was turned in for the weekly payroll. It was about 10:00 a.m. and I was praying, "God, what shall I do? Shall I go down to the office, or what shall I do?" Right about then Mr. Gray came walking down my isle at a very fast pace. As he walked by my bench I turned and said "Oh,

Mr. Gray." He said, "Yes, what is it?" I said, "Remember the agreement we had when you hired me?" He said "No, what was it?" I said "You said if my work was satisfactory you would pay me 25 cents an hour over union scale on my fourth pay check." He said "Oh, yes, just a minute." He went over and conversed with the foreman for a minute. He came back and said, "It will be on your pay check," and he walked off. Thank you Jesus! Thank You Holy Spirit! The 25 cents an hour was on my pay check, just as he said.

Monday morning the union steward didn't waste any time coming to me to ask if I got the 25 cents an hour over scale on my pay check. I said "Yes." He said "You're the new steward." I said "Oh no, I'm not." The steward said, "We have been trying to get a 5 cents an hour raise and can't get it. You come in here and get 25 cents over scale on your fourth pay check. We have had a meeting and voted you in as our new steward." I said "Oh, no I'm not. Not on your life." There wasn't much more said about it for the next five months.

About that time the union contract was going to be up. The foreman came to me and asked me to move my work bench right at the top of the back stairs. I worked on the second floor. I worked at the top of the stairs for about a month. On a Friday the paymaster came and gave me my last two pay checks. In other words, he laid me off. He told me to gather up all my tools, go down the back stairs and say nothing to no one, which I did. He was very emphatic. I then went to the union hall and registered on the "out of work" list. They said they didn't have a job for me, but they wanted me to walk the picket line in front of the Chevrolet garage. I carried the sign for two days. In the meantime I had registered at the unemployment office.

You will soon see how the Holy Spirit had His hand on my getting laid off. I always welcome being laid off if the Holy Spirit has something better for me. While I was working at Walarus Manufacturing Company I remodeled our house. I built new kitchen cabinets and new wardrobes in the bedrooms, with drawers along the bottom of the wardrobes. Luella, my wife, loved them.

I had registered at the unemployment office. I thought my union days were over, but as we will see the Holy Spirit had other ideas.

1 Timothy 5:8
But if any provide not for his own, and specially for those of his own house, he hath denied the faith, and is worse than an infidel.

HEY BOY, YOU WANTA GO THE SHOW?

Mr. Sawal was a German immigrant. He had opened up an iron scrap yard in Decatur and was making a lot of money. He started buying up old commercial buildings, remodeling them and renting them out. He ran an ad in the paper for a carpenter and I answered the ad.

("Remember the only carpenter experience I had was in the cabinet shop!")

Mr. Sawal hired me. He bought two buildings just two blocks from where I had been working. In one building we built three large round vats for storing grape wine. The other building had been rented to State Farm Insurance Company. I was laying flooring for the office building. I was whistling and singing praises while I was working. Mr. Sawal came up to me and said, "**Hey Boy, you wanta go the show**?" I was startled. I looked up and said "**No**, I don't want to go to a show. In his German brogue he said, "**Well boy**, get to work then." I said to myself, "What was that all about?"

I was laying and nailing the flooring as fast as I could, while still doing a good job. I began feeling God's presence again, so I started whistling and singing again. I could have been singing "The Glory of His Presence" because I surely did feel God's Holy Spirit around me. I continued to lay and nail flooring and started singing and whistling. Here came Mr. Sawal again. He said "**Hey boy**, I though I asked you, you wanta go the show?" I said (kind of indignantly) "**No**, I don't want to go to a show." "Well, get to work then!" he said. "What's the matter with this guy?" I thought to myself.

I must have been doing a good job because everyone else had been laid off. I continued to lay the flooring and feeling the strong presence of the Holy Spirit, I started whistling and singing again. To my amazement Mr. Sawal was yelling at me in his German brogue "**Hey boy, I thought I asked you, you wanta go the show?**" I was very indignant. "**No I don't wanta go the show.**" Well, it finally dawned on me what the problem was. Mr. Sawal didn't want me to sing or whistle. So I complied.

I want you to pay close attention to how the Holy Spirit works. I went home from work one day and my wife said that the union hall had called. They wanted me to come up to the hall. My faith went through the floor. I thought they had found out that I was working non-union. After all, the union had not found me a job, so I took a non-union job. I had a family to care for. God's Word burns in my mind and heart. Because I love my wife and family.

I repeat:

1 Timothy 5:8

But if any provide not for his own, and specially for those of his own house, he hath denied the faith, and is worse than an infidel.

I think the verse needed to be repeated for some of you who are reading this book.

The next morning I went to the union hall and met with the business agent. (B.A. as he is known.) The B.A. said they had gotten my job back at Walarus Manufacturing Company. "**What?**" I said. "They fired me!" (I want you to take notice. Unbeknownst to me The Holy Spirit was working for me. Pay close attention!) I said "I'm not going to go back and work for them." The B.A. said "That's what the strike was all about, getting your job back." "**Strike?**" I said. "I didn't know they were on strike." Now remember I was working just two blocks from where they were striking. I was prompted to say "You have other jobs you could send me out on!" The B.A. said real sheepishly, "Well, I guess I could." So he sent me out on a house job. The house job was on Lake Decatur. The house was being built for the Chevrolet dealer. Here is where the Holy Spirit went to work for me again. You see, the cabinet shops wage scale is half as much as the men working "on the outside" got. I know you ask "Why?" They say that cabinet men get to work year round and the men working on the outside miss a lot of work because of bad weather.

THE SWEARING FOREMAN

Decatur has a large railroad switching yard where they make up trains going all directions in our country. They were changing all of the manual switches over to automated switches. God's Holy Spirit wanted to test my patience with a humbling experience. The union sent me out to work on this job. The foreman's name was Boman. I do not remember very many of the foremen's names that I have worked for, but boy I sure remember this man. I had to listen really good in order to understand what he was saying, because he used more swear words than he did the English language. His father worked there also. I felt very sorry for him. Boman swore at him the same way he swore at the rest of us. His father was dying of prostrate cancer. I was very thankful for

72

the job despite the unfortunate conditions. I worked there about four or five months. I felt that God had another job for me. I want you to take notice. This is the way the Holy Spirit works for me, and He wants to do the same for you.

When I got to the union meeting I was directed to sit down by this gentleman. I said hello and sat down by him. There was something said about where I was raised. I said "On a farm." He said that he was raised on a farm also. Without hesitation he said "Are you working?" I said, "Yes" and I told him what I was putting up with. He said "I am a foreman on the Stally grain elevator, with 142 silos. He was a farmer and I was a farmer. It was easy to converse with him. He said "I have a job for you. I will get a work order for you. You report out on my job Monday morning." I said "OK, thank you very much."

You see how the Holy Spirit was working for me again! I continued to work at the railroad switching yard the rest of the week. Friday right on cue, about 2 o'clock Mr. Boman came up to where I was working on one of the switches. As usual he started cursing a "blue streak" at me. I waited until I could get a word in edge wise. I said "Mr. Boman, I would like to have both my checks today because this will be my last day here." Boy did he let me have it with both barrels. He said "You can't quit me. You are my best man." When he calmed down I said "Mr. Boman, would you like to know why I am quitting?" He said "Yes, you @#%*^." I said "For what you are doing right now." He said "What's that?" "All that swearing you are doing," I replied. He said, "If you will not quit I will never swear again." "I am sorry Mr. Boman, but I already have another job." He said "OK" and went and got my two paychecks.

I met Mr. Boman briefly some 20 years later and as I walked up to him he said, "Well, hello there Gilbert." I don't know if he quit swearing.

THE 142 SLIP FORM SILO JOB

Monday morning I reported to the Stally Elevator job, and to the foreman. He put me to work with the other men building the slip forms and platform that would rise slowly as they poured the concrete in the silo forms. They tried to pour six inches per hour. A week or two after I started to work there the foreman came to me and said "Gilbert, I have just the job for you. It pays time and a half." Under my breath, I said "Thank You Jesus, thank You Holy Spirit!" "Gilbert, I want you to pick any one of these men you would like to work with." I said, "I just want men that like to work. How would that be?" He pointed out a middle aged man that had been a farmer. This man was a good man to work with. I worked on the elevator for about one and a half years, at time and a half.

I started in the cabinet shop at $1.50 + .25. This was 1948. Wages were very low. The Holy Spirit moved me to the outside work. My wages doubled. Then the Holy Spirit moved me to the elevator job at time and a half. I only take credit for being sensitive to the Holy Spirit and recognizing when He was doing something for me and my family, or when to back off when I was out of God's will in my life.

The men on most jobs will tell you to slow down. They will say "What are you trying to do, kill the job?" I would say "Oh, I'm sorry." I would slow my work down. Then I would gradually speed up again. As the elevator job was finishing up they started laying men off each week, but I was not one of them. There were several foremen on the job and they were the last ones to be laid off. They laid most of the foremen off before they laid me off. A foreman gets .50 more per hour over union scale. I was making more than the foreman was making. Prayer is the open line to heaven that connects us to the source of all power.

Exodus 4:15

And thou shalt speak unto him, and put words in his mouth: and I will be with thy mouth, and with his mouth, and WILL TEACH YOU WHAT YE SHALL DO.

Chapter 7

1 Corinthians 2:5
That your faith should not stand in the wisdom of
men, but in the power of God.

Read this Scripture again. This is what the average Christian does. They put their faith in men and their education, and not the power of God.

LEARNING THE CALIFORNIA HOUSE PRODUCTION SYSTEM

When I asked God to help me train so I could go into business for myself, I had to be sensitive to the leading of the Holy Spirit. I was not happy with the type of training I was receiving in Decatur, Illinois. I knew that in California they built houses on a production system. I felt that I must move my family to California and learn their production system.

So, in 1951 I moved my family to Van Nuys, California. I worked on a few 'Class A' jobs. ('Class A' is considered commercial construction work.) That is not what I came to California for. I came to California to learn the house production system. Orange County was just starting to break wide open with housing tracts. They were building 200, 300, even 500 tract houses. I had to get in on this. This is what I came to California for.

I moved my family to Brea California and we attended the Brea Four Square Church. Rev. Loren Wood was the pastor. My wife Luella played the piano and I taught a Sunday School class. My first job in California was a door hanging job that I called "Don't Say Skill-Saw." That's in another chapter. I then went from job to job, learning the California production system. I always worked with another man. The union calls it 'the buddy system.' When we would finish up a job I would head for the union hall and put my name on the "out of work" list. I would then go and register at the unemployment office. This was a safety net. When the roll was called the next morning and my name came up, I took whatever job came up. Other carpenters were picky, so they were out of work a lot of the time.

When I would take the jobs that I had never done before I could hear the Holy Spirit saying "Atta boy! Atta boy! That's the way to do it. I am right here with you." As you've already seen in this book thus far, this Bible verse is my theme:

Philippians 4:13
I can do all things through Christ which strength-
eneth me.

Another theme that I have, and practice is:

If you can do it, I can do it!
Never say No.

I keep track of how much time it took for each phase, and how many square feet were in that phase of the houses. I took jobs setting foundation form. I got a job laying floor joists, laying sub flooring, framing or stacking rafters, or laying ceiling joists, and so forth. I kept track of the time. When I was at the union hall for a job and my name was called, I always said "I'll take that job!" (My theme…Thinking that if I did not please the foreman he could always lay me off, with a days pay, of course!) I was looking for a job when I got that one but, I never did get laid off.

Exodus 4:15
And thou shalt speak unto him, and put words in his mouth: and I will be with thy mouth, and with his mouth, and will teach you what ye shall do.

Many of the construction workers say they specialize in different phases of the house. Well, they are out of work most of the time. I have known men that have been in the construction trade for fifteen or twenty years and they only had eight or ten years retirement in. I have had people ask me what kind of carpenter work I did. I would say "I am a carpenter." "Yes, but what phase do you do?" I would answer, "I start with the plans and then the foundation and when I am finished I move them into their new house." They would say "Oh, I see." "In other words, I do it all." "Wow" they would respond "I never met a man that can do it all."

I worked at different times with apprentice carpenters. Two of them went to state competition. One was a college graduate. He had majored in architecture, but he still had to come up through the apprenticeship in the union. *Remember he is being trained by man that has less than a 7th grade education.* **This is what the Holy Spirit did for me and He will do it for you also, if you will open your heart up to Him. Don't hold some of it back.** I helped this apprentice sharpen his skills so he could enter the state competition. He thought he was really big stuff after he came back from the state competition.

We were working on a condominium job that had two recreation buildings that had been assigned to us to build. We were just about finished framing the walls when this young man said, "I am going to take the plans and go cut the rafters." I said "You can't cut the rafters off of the plans." He didn't ask why not. He said, "Yes, I can." I said "They won't fit if you do." He said, "Yes, they will. " I tried to explain to him that we had to finish framing the building and then take the measurements off of the building, but his college education had gotten to him. (I never did tell anyone that I had a 7th grade education until after God told me to write this book. Not even my children. It was between God and I.)

I let him get the rafters ready to cut and went one more time and tried to explain why he needed to take the measurements off of the framed buildings, but he wouldn't listen. The rafters for these buildings were big beams. He gave me no choice. I had to go to the foreman to get him to stop because he would have ruined those rafter beams. He didn't get laid off, but I thought he would.

I cannot put in writing how much I relied on the Holy Spirit to guide me and teach me while on the job.

After I worked in Orange County for a while I found out that I could go out and get my own jobs. I liked this because I could negotiate my wages. Thank You Holy Spirit! From this time on I received from .50 to $2.00 per hour above scale.

I teamed up with a Baptist man from Texas named John Shelden. He was a good worker and had worked on all phases of construction. I believe that the Holy Spirit teamed me up with John. I did not have to put up with smoking and swearing. That made us a good team. I felt the Holy Spirit nudge me to do all of the wage negotiating. We were always the last ones to be laid off on the jobs. Thank You Holy Spirit! I worked with John until I went into my own business.

After I went in business for myself in Belleville, Illinois, my wife and I came to California on vacation. We stopped by the Shelden's. Mrs. Shelden said that John would get upset at me sometimes and would want to quit working with me. She would tell him "You're not going to quit working with Gilbert. He is always working. You have never worked steady before." Thank You Jesus! God and His Holy Spirit kept us working. God helps those who help themselves. God will not send His Holy Spirit to help a lazy people.

Proverbs 20:13
Love not sleep, lest thou come to poverty; open thine eyes, and thou shalt be satisfied with bread.

Hebrews 6:12
THAT YE BE NOT SLOTHFUL, but followers of them who through faith and patience inherit the promises.

These are warnings to us about laziness. The lazier a man is, the more he intends to do tomorrow.

I never worried about getting laid off before the job was finished because I always tried to be the best worker on the job, with the Holy Spirit's help. I made sure I was not a show-off, just a good, steady worker. I made sure that my work was not shoddy.

Hebrews 5:11 (L.B.V.)
There is much more I would like to say along these lines, but you don't seem to listen, so its hard to make you understand.

Chapter 8

Hebrews 5:11 (L.B.V.)
There is much more I would like to say along these lines, but you don't seem to listen, so its hard to make you understand.

Psalm 71:16
I will go in the strength of the Lord GOD: I will make mention of thy righteousness, even of thine only.

DON'T SAY SKILL-SAW

A fter I had read my Bible for about 15 minutes and prayed for about the same amount of time I headed for the carpenter's union hall.

Judges 5:3-b
I will sing unto the Lord. I will sing praise to God of Israel.

On the way, I sang and worshipped God and talked to Jesus in my heavenly language. At the union hall I started to sign the "Out of Work" register. I was shocked. **There were 441 names on the "Out of Work" register!** That's right, I said **441** names on the register. My name made 442. There were 28 jobs written on the black board. I said "Lord, is one of those jobs mine?" A voice in me said "Yes." My faith was very low at that point. The secretary started calling the roll at 8:00 a.m. As the roll was called and your name was called, you could choose the job that you wanted, or you could pass. By the time the secretary had called 50 names, all of the jobs were gone, **but one.**

I said "Lord, is that my job?" A voice in me said "Yes, that's your job." It was a door hanging job, and I had never hung a door in my life. The secretary was still calling the names; 200, 300, the job was still on the board. He had now called over 430 names, and I was nervous as a *cat on a hot tin roof.* I could hear a voice in me saying "Take it, take it; I am with you." I said "I sure hope so, because I'm going to make a real fool out of myself if You're not." My number was called. I said, "I'll take that job." The secretary asked, "Can you hang doors?" I said "Yes Sir" (with as much confidence in my voice as I could muster.)

At this point I want you to notice how the secretary worded the question. He did not ask, "Are you a door hanger?" He asked, "Can you hang doors?"

I was not put in a position to be tempted to lie. The Holy Spirit was working for me when He caused the secretary to ask the question in the right way. Believing God's promises, I got my work order and left the hall. The union allowed you two hours to get to your new job. I said "Lord, thank You for this new job, but now what do I do?" The Holy Spirit said to me, "There is a man waiting for you in Fullerton who will teach you how to hang doors."

The union hall was in Tustin, California. A voice said to me, "Go to Commonwealth Avenue and go west, and I will tell you were to turn."

I headed for Fullerton, worshipping God and singing God's praises all the way. When I got to Fullerton I began driving down Commonwealth, as I had been instructed. A voice said "Turn left at the next corner and go to the end of the street. The man will be there waiting for you."

As I turned the corner I could hardly believe my eyes. I could see a man standing in the doorway, leaning against the door jamb with his arms crossed. I said, "Is that the man who will teach me to hang doors?" The voice in my head said, "Yes." I am telling you, I almost came apart.

Ephesians 3:20
Now unto him that is able to do exceeding abundantly above all that we ask or think, according to the power that worketh in us...

As I am writing this, that same warm thrilling feeling is going through my body. I walked up to the man and asked, "Are you a door hanger?" He said, "Yes." I said, "I have a job hanging doors and I don't know how to hang them. Would you show me how?" He said, "Sure, come on in."

This man spent over one hour showing me the method and skill of hanging doors: How to scribe the doors, how to build a table to hold the doors while I would cut the thick edges off, and level the edges with the skill-saw set on a 5 degree angle. (Notice I said 'skill-saw'; remember that.)

He showed me how to smooth the saw marks out with one thin cut using the electric planer. (Now remember, one of the main tools was the skill-saw.) I thanked the door hanger man and headed for my job out in Buena Park, California. I never saw the man again, but I think if I had gone back and tried to find him I would not have been able to find him, because I think he was one of **God's angels**. No man would have been leaning against a door jamb at 9:00 a.m. He would have been working. If he would have been an ordinary carpenter

– door–hanger, and I would have approached him and told him I took a job hanging doors, but didn't know how to hang them, he would have said, **"You crazy fool, why did you take the job if you didn't know how to hang doors? Go get someone else to teach you."**

This is why I am convinced that he had to be an angel. As he showed me, he was very kind and understanding. I kept saying all the way to the job, "Thank You Lord, thank You Jesus, thank You Holy Spirit, thank You God." I know that the Three-In-One was concerned about His child.

John 14:26
But the Comforter, which is the Holy Ghost, whom the Father will send in my name, he shall teach you all things, and bring all things to your remembrance, whatsoever I have said unto you.

Arriving at my new job, I gave my work order to the superintendent. He was a big man who towered over me. He looked at my work order and asked, "Alright, what tools do you need?" That struck me as funny because all union contractors were required to furnish all the power tools; the carpenters would furnish the hand tools. I started to tell him that I would need a skill-saw, but just as I opened my mouth a voice beside me said very quickly, **"Don't say skill-saw."** I became dazed because that was the first tool that I would be using to build the table with. I knew the Holy Spirit had been talking to me earlier, but this voice was not inside, in my thoughts, it was on my right side like someone was standing beside me. I stuttered. "Uh...uh...." The voice said again, **"Don't say skill-saw."** Again I hesitated and the voice said it a third time, really emphatically, **"DON'T SAY SKILL-SAW."** I told the superintended what power tools that I would need: Electric drill, a router and a planer, but I left the skill-saw out. Then the superintendent said, "OK, you've got the job." Now I was dumbfounded for sure. I said, "Sir, could I ask you a question?" He said, "Sure." I said, "Why did you question me about the tools that I would need the way that you did?" His answer was this: "Well, since you ask I will tell you. The union sent two other men out here and the first thing they asked for was a skill-saw, and I won't have one used on my doors." "But sir," I said, "I will need a skill-saw to build the work table." He said, "No problem, you can use one to do that."

I had six hours left to work that day. I built the table and sharpened the router and planer blades (which I had never done before.) The doors were three feet wide, seven feet tall and two inches thick, and made of solid core birch. They were heavy as lead. I hung five doors that day.

The planer was a small one. It would cut no more than one sixteenth to one eighth of an inch at a time. About quitting time the superintendent came by and said, "Well, you didn't get much done today, but we'll give it *hell* tomorrow, won't we?" I said, "yes sir," but the most that I could do was five doors a day the rest of the job, and I worked just as fast as I could. The fourth day I saw the union business agent and the superintendent looking over the doors that I had hung. I thought, "Oh boy, what's wrong now?" The business agent came over to where I was working and asked for my name and telephone number. I asked, "Why do you need that?" He said "We don't have anyone in our hall that can hang doors as good as you do." Wow! I almost thanked the Holy Spirit out loud.

They started laying off men, but I was not one of them. As usual I stayed until the end of the job. Thank You Holy Spirit!

The superintendent asked me to go to the next job with him. I turned him down. His new job was too far for me to drive. (I try to get jobs not more than 20 minutes from my house so that I can get home to my family as soon as possible.)

The Holy Spirit has intervened for me many times. Thank You Lord.

We sing the song, "Holy Spirit I Need Thee," but we don't seem to recognize that He longs for us to need Him, so He can help us in our daily activities.

John 15:7
If ye abide in me, and my words abide in you, ye shall ask what ye will, and it shall be done unto you.

Chapter 9

---⊛⊛⊛---

Joshua 1:9
**Have not I commanded thee? Be strong and of a
good courage; be not afraid, neither be thou dismayed:
for the LORD THY GOD IS WITH THEE WHITHER
SO EVER THOU GOEST.**

THE KNOTT'S BERRY FARM
FOREMANS JOB

When I finished a job on Friday evening, on Monday morning as my routine, I would pray for fifteen minutes always asking Jesus to reveal His Word to me, (just like He was sitting there reading to me) and make the Bible come alive. I would read the Bible for about fifteen minutes. (Try it, it works!) I then would eat a good hearty breakfast. Just before I left home I would tell my wife goodbye. She would say "I will tell you goodbye, because I know you won't be back today until you have a job." **She was right**.

Proverbs 20:13 speaks to a common malady, or bad habit:

Proverbs 20:13
Do not love sleep, lest you come to poverty; Open your eyes, *and* you will be satisfied with bread. (N.K.J.V.)

That is a warning against laziness. The lazier a man is, the more he intends to do tomorrow. Don't allow yourself to fall into the Proverb 20:13 category. Get out there and "*get it!*" You sure can't do it laying in bed.

Philippians 4:13
I can do all things through Christ which strengtheneth me.

I then would head for the union hall. On my way I prayed and talked to God in my heavenly language. When I got to the hall I found out that Knott's Berry Farm had an order in for 22 men. *Something* said to me (*like the Holy Spirit!*) "They are going to need a good foreman. **Go out there and get that job.**"

I did as I was instructed. I went out to the superintendent's trailer. I walked in and introduced myself. I said, "I see you are hiring a crew of men today from the union hall." He said "yes." He was working at his desk and never looked up. I said "then you are going to need a good foreman." Not looking up he said, "no, we don't need one." **"Oh, yes you do, you need me"** I said. He stopped what he was doing and looked up. "Why do I need you? Because most foremen just point their men to the job. I don't do that. I make sure they don't make mistakes." He said **"look over those plans laying on the drawing board."** At the same time there was a big crane out beside the trailer with two men trying to set a ride motor. (That motor weighed over 50 tons. It had been shipped in from Germany. It was a motor for a ride called the **Lupo Plane**.) The two men had been struggling and trying to set that motor for over an hour. I told the superintendent that

I didn't understand what those men were doing. **"I can set that motor in less than 10 minutes."** He stopped working and looked up and stared at me. (I'll bet he was thinking, "what kind of a *superman* are you anyway.") He didn't know that the Holy Spirit was speaking through me.

It wasn't long until one of the men came in and said that they needed to call the union hall for two more men. (I want you to take notice right here. I say that the Holy Spirit had been working for me. He would not allow those men to set that motor without my help. He wanted to seal that job for me.)

Romans 8:31
If God be for us who can be against us.

Matthew 19:26
But Jesus beheld them, and said unto them, With men this is impossible; but with God all things are possible.

The superintendent said "Gilbert said that he can set that motor, so let him do it." The men said, OK. I went out to help the men and it only took me about five minutes to set it. I went back in the office trailer and said "I got the motor set." The superintendent said "keep looking over those plans." He never did say that he would hire me, but I knew that the Holy Spirit had sealed my job in his mind.

I have a rule that God asked me to use when selling something, or being hired. You've heard it before in this book, but I want to remind you again, if you ask someone a question **"THE ONE THAT SPEAKS FIRST LOSES."** Don't ever forget this rule.

Well, at last the field superintendent came into the trailer. The superintendent said to him, "take Gilbert out to the front gate and give him half of the men that are coming from the union hall. The field super just stood there. He didn't want me hired. He wanted one of his cronies to be the foreman. The superintendent said "give Gilbert half of the men and have him build the trusses for the entry gate." The Holy Spirit was working for me again. I don't remember when I went into the union hall to get my work order, but when I did go, they wanted to know how I got the foreman's job because they said they had been trying to get one of their men on as a foreman out at Knott's Berry Farm. I did just what Jesus would have done. I said nothing.

The field super took me to the front gate that they were building, and introduced me to another foreman. About that time the 22 men started coming from the union hall. The other foreman and his men were building the lower part of the front gate. My men and I were to build the upper part of the gate. He had been instructed to give me 11 men. He started calling off names. He called three names and I stopped him. I called him over to one side and said, "if you give me one more man like these, I am quitting."

(I knew that it was the Holy Spirit that instructed me to say that. I would not have done that in myself. I would have taken those men. You see the Holy Spirit had given me the wisdom to be able to look at a man and tell if he liked to work or not.)

The foreman said, "Oh no, you pick the men you want." I chose the rest of my 11 men. The field super took me into the construction shed and gave me a set of plans. My men and I were to build the trusses for the entry gate.

When you visit Knott's Berry Farm and you go through the front gates, look up at the trusses and think of me and my men. It is a beautiful sight to behold.

The first thing I did was split my men into two groups. I had the men start building gigs so we could build the trusses on production. We had been working about two or three hours on the truss gigs when the superintendent and Mary

Knott came by. The superintendent said "what's going on here. You haven't got one truss made up." I said, "just give us a little more time and you will see what happens." After we built the gigs the trusses started coming out on a production line. After we got the trusses built a crane lifted them in place. The super told me that they had figured three days time for building each truss and we built them in one and a half days each. The superintendent asked me to split my men into two groups and pick a man out to be the foreman. I would work one crew in the day time, and one crew in the evening. He said I could work as many hours as I wanted to work. I worked there three years helping to rebuild the park.

I tell you about my job at Knott's Berry Farm so you can see how God and the Holy Spirit worked for me. **The Holy Spirit wants to do the same for you,** if you will humble yourself before God and absorb His Word and apply His promises. God is longing for you to do it. I did not stand around and watch my men work, or visit with someone like other foremen do. I saw to it that their material was always at their fingertips, and if one of them had a problem I was there to help them. The men said I was the best foreman they had ever worked for. After that job when I would meet with any of the men they would ask me when I was going to get another foreman's job because they wanted to work for me. I didn't feel led to be a foreman because I could get as much as $2.00 per hour over scale working as a carpenter. Most superintendents and foremen make less money than carpenters make. They say it is worth something to get to be a foreman. So they take less money. NOT ME!

Philippians 2:13
For it is God which worketh in you both to will
and to do of his good pleasure.

93

Chapter 10

———— ∞∞∞ ————

Exodus 4:15
And thou shalt speak unto him, and put words in his mouth: and I will be with thy mouth, and with his mouth, and will teach you what ye shall do.

THE RAFTER-CUTTING JOB

Sheldon and I worked as a carpenter team. We had been hired onto a job as rafter stackers. We always bargained our hourly wage. We were getting $1.50 per hour over average journeymen's wage on this job. We were the third team to be hired.

There was an "ex-airforce fighter pilot Major" cutting the rafters for the three rafter-stacking crews. He was a very good rafter cutter.

Again, the Holy Spirit went to work for me. After we had been working on this job a few days the foreman came to me and asked if I could cut rafters. Of course I said "yes."

Philippians 4:13
I can do all things through Christ which strengtheneth me.

Exodus 4:15b
...and I will teach you what ye shall do.

But why did he ask me? Why didn't he ask one of the other rafter-stackers? To me there was only one answer! The Holy Spirit was there watching over me and directing the mind of the foreman. The Holy Spirit knew that when I went into business for myself I would need to know how to cut rafters!

The foreman said that he wanted me to start cutting rafters the next morning, but the question was: Why did he ask me and not Mr. Sheldon? Mr. Sheldon was older than I was. It should have been obvious that he would have had more experience than I, or one of the other rafter-men had. I believe, like I said before, that the Holy Spirit influenced him.

I went home and told Luella what had happened. She asked "Have you ever cut rafters before?" I said "no." I know that **if I believed God's promises then I could cut those rafters**, but my faith waned. I stayed up late that night trying to figure out how to cut them. All I knew about rafters was the little bit I had learned while working with Mr. Sheldon stacking rafters, and that wasn't much. The next day I felt impressed to start cutting rafters next to the other rafter-cutter. What does that verse say in:

Exodus 4:15
"I will be with thy mouth, and with his mouth, and will teach you what ye shall do."

I was shaking in my boots, but I believed God's Word. As I was setting up, the other rafter-cutter could see that I was not an experienced rafter-cutter. He came over and asked "Have you ever cut rafters before?" I said "No." *The Holy Spirit was at work again. Thank You, Lord!* He said "Let me show you how to set up to cut rafters." He then showed me the rafter-cutting book he had. He told me where to buy the book, so I bought one that evening.

This man did not need to teach me how to cut rafters, but he seemed to be eager to do it. Two days later he was laid off. Boy, did I feel bad. He could hardly talk because his throat was cut out from drinking whisky and most of all, he was a veteran "Major" from the air force. He had flown many missions.

I was now on my own, just me and the Holy Spirit to help me. I was fortunate. The Holy Spirit arranged it so the first few roofs were what we call, *shotgun roofs.* In other words, they were straight roofs. They were easy roofs to cut. No problems. (Remember, I was cutting for three crews!)

Then the fun started. I had roofs that had a lot of different kinds of offsets in them. And you know, I didn't make one mistake!

There was however, one professor that had come out from St. Louis University. He had taught construction at the University and he thought he could make more money doing carpentry work in California. He was stacking roofs on this job. It so happened he got one of the roofs that I had cut that had a lot of different offsets in it (hips and valleys.) The professor couldn't put the roof together, so he went to the foreman and told him the roof would not fit the way I had cut it. I wondered if he thought he should have gotten my job. He told the foreman that he couldn't make the roof fit. He would have to re-cut some of it. The foreman came right over to me and said, "Go see what is the matter with the roof you cut for the professor." I went down and checked it and it was cut right. The professor was not putting it together right. I told the professor, "If you have any trouble again, come to me; don't go to the foreman."

I was trying to protect him so he wouldn't look bad, and get laid off.

Well, it wasn't long until he got another roof that was all cut up, with a lot of hips and valley and offsets in it. What did he do? He headed for the foreman again. The foreman told me to go find out what was the matter with the professor's roof. This time he couldn't make a filler fit. I laid it in place, picked up a 2x4 and propped it in place. I told him a second time, "don't go to the foreman if you have any problems." Well, within two or three days he went to the foreman again instead of coming to me, and the foreman laid him off.

The moral of this story is: Don't go to the foreman if you have a question. Try to ask one of your fellow workers if you have a question about your work. Most foremen don't have a clue how to do the job that you are doing. All most foremen do is point you to the job they want you to do, and if you don't know how to do the job, they will lay you off.

I didn't know how to cut rafters either, but my friend the Holy Spirit did. He taught me just like He says in the Bible that He would. He will do it for you too, if you will do what His Word tells you to do.

Those were the last rafters I cut until I went into business for myself. But I learned to cut them well by being sensitive to the Holy Spirit and by using my faith in Him.

Romans 12:3b
..according as God hath dealt to every man the measure of faith.

Chapter 11

———— ∞∞∞ ————

Ecclesiastes 8:1
Who is as the wise man? and who knoweth the
interpretation of a thing? a man's wisdom maketh
his face to shine, and the boldness of his face shall be
changed.

THE ARCHITECT

It was now 1955. I had been studying the California house production system for four years. I felt that I knew every phase of the system. If I was going to be a contractor I should build a house and see if I could make some money on it.

Luella and I spent all of our spare time going from one tract to the next studying the designs, and decorating. We felt that we were ready to build our first house. I had a folder with pictures and a floor plan I had cut out of a magazine. But I wanted some changes made on the plans, and changes on the elevation. Since it had to pass the building department inspection I would need to take it to an architect. I took the ideas that I had to an architect that had been recommended to me. We agreed on a price, so I left my ideas with him. The architect said to come back in two weeks and he would have the plans ready. I went back as we had agreed. The house plans looked terrible. He said he didn't think he could draw what I wanted. I could see in my mind exactly what I wanted on that paper. He said he would see what he could do. After three trips I was very disgusted. The plans were worse than ever. I asked him if I could pay him what we had agreed on if he would give me the paper skin he was drawing on. He said that he had never done that before, but he would do it this time. The Holy Spirit was in control again for me. **He wanted me to draw those plans. He wanted to develop another talent in me.**

I took the skin paper home and got an ink pen and a ruler. I then drew on that paper what I could see in my mind. I took the plans to the Brea Building and Planning Department. They made three minor changes on the plans and then stamped them. **I was shocked.** He then gave me my building permit. I wanted to jump up and down and yell *"Glory Hallelujah, thank You Jesus, thank You Holy Spirit*! **I was living on cloud nine.** I had no idea that I could draw plans. I would soon become the DESIGNER and BUILDER of THE STORY BOOK HOMES, unbeknownst to me at this time. This will be told in another chapter. In the meantime Luella and I were interviewing subdividers. We were able to get one to agree to subordinate a lot to us. That means that he put the lot in our name without us paying him any money until we sold the house. The lot we got was in the best subdivision in Brea. **The Holy Spirit was right there with us putting words in my mouth and causing the subdivider to think in our favor.**

Mark 13:11b
"..take no thought beforehand what ye shall speak, neither do ye premeditate: but whatsoever shall be given you in that hour, <u>that speak ye: for it is not ye that speak, but the Holy Ghost."</u>

My folks loaned us $500 (to help pay for some labor) and because the subdivider subordinated the lot to us we were able to go to the bank in Brea and get a loan for the building materials. I built the house on schedule and sold it for a nice profit.

We went back and visited the people that bought the house some years later. They said they loved the house and had no intention of selling it. It was a 3 bedroom, 2 ½ bath with 2 fireplaces. The den walls were covered with pithy cypress. The door and trim had a furniture finish on it. The roof was covered with shake shingles. There was rough siding on the garage and the front of the house. It is a lovely house. The next chapter is the VISION.

Romans 8:31
What shall we then say to these things? If God be for us, who can be against us?

Chapter 12

---∞∞∞---

Hebrews 11:6
But without faith it is impossible to please him:
for he that cometh to God must believe that he is, and
that he is a rewarder of them that diligently seek him.

THE VISION

I had proven to myself that I could build a house on the California house production system, and make money on it.

I first came to California in the spring of 1945. We went back to Illinois in 1946, came back in 1951 and it was now 1956. I had been back in California five years. I now knew how much time to took to do every phase in the building of a house, per square foot, for the labor. But the question was, where should I go into business? If I went into business in California I would have to get a contractor's license and the plans would have to go through the Building and Planning Department to be approved. The lots would have to be approved and inspected also. If I went back to Illinois I could hang out a shingle with my name on it and start building a house. So I had been praying about it, and one night I was laying in bed praying and meditating about what we should do. (The wall at the foot of our bed was a blank wall without a window in it.)

I was laying there with my eyes open, when all of a sudden up along the top of the wall and about thirty inches down, **four squares lit up in different colors.** When I saw the *writing on the wall* I thought I was dreaming even through I knew I was awake. (It was like when Peter was in prison and the angel came and woke him up; he thought he was dreaming.)

Each square had writing in it. I can see it now as if I were there. Although all the squares were different colors the lettering was all black.

- **BLOCK #1:** Go back to Springfield, Illinois and I will show you where to go into business.

- **BLOCK #2:** Draw some plans. Show them to the subdividers. **They will subordinate the lots to you.**

- **BLOCK #3:** Show the subcontractors your plans. Ask them to carry their part of the job until the house is sold. **They will do it for you.**

- **BLOCK #4:** INCORPORATE. Name your company "BETTER BUILDERS DESIGNERS and BUILDERS OF THE STORY BOOK HOMES"

I was stunned! But why should I have been? I was living day by day on God's promises and was sure that the Holy Spirit was working on my behalf.

Matthew 17:20
...If ye have faith as a grain of mustard seed, ye shall say unto this mountain, Remove hence to yonder

place; and it shall remove; and nothing shall be impossible unto you.

The way I saw it I was moving mountains. I told my mother and father what my plans were and they said, "why, that will take at least $150,000 to do that." I said, "God showed me how to go into business with just the money for the house labor." My dad said, "I sure hope you know what you are doing. Besides, we are in a recession." This was during the time of President Dwight Eisenhower years and everyone said that we were in a big recession, but the Holy Spirit had me blinded to it. Everyone I talked to would tell me about the big recession that we were in, but that didn't seem to bother me. I opened my Bible and read that God would even *give me the heathen, if I ask him.*

Psalm 2:8
Ask of me, and I shall give thee the heathen for thine inheritance, and the uttermost parts of the earth for thy possession.

How could you or I lose with such promises as these that God has given us?

2 Chronicles 32:8a
With him is an arm of flesh; but with us is the LORD our God to help us, and to fight our battles. And the people rested themselves upon the words of Hezekiah king of Judah.

SQUARE #1: The first square said to move back to Illinois. Our pastor and friends said that we were making a big mistake. But I was sure that we were not. I was impressed not to tell anyone about my bedroom experience until now because they would have said that I was lying. We called the

Mayflower moving company. They moved our furniture and I loaded my tools, washer and dryer in a 4x8 steel farm trailer that I paid $75 for in 1951. We said goodbye to California.

Luella and our four girls and I had a good trip back to Illinois. But as usual, I drove straight through. Loading the heavy things and driving straight through I hurt my heart. My heart was beating very fast and then very slow. I went to a doctor in Springfield and he gave me some medicine that seemed to help, but more about my heart in a later chapter.

My father had a small farm out by Mechanicsburg, about five miles from Springfield. He let us move into the house until we found out where I was going into business. I soon found that Springfield was not the place. I went over to Decatur, forty miles east of Springfield. This is where we were living when we moved to California in 1951. I looked the town over and something said to me "this is not the place." I went fifty miles north to Bloomington. I looked the town over and something said "this is not the place."

These towns had 50,000 to 100,000 people living in them. We had some friends that lived in Belleville, Illinois that we wanted to visit, so we went to Belleville. Belleville is 100 miles south of Springfield up on the bluff from East St. Louis. Our friends were Bill and Beth Woods. It so happened that their whole family was in the building trade. The building business was booming there, so it seemed. Bill said there was room for all of us. He said "come on down." Scott Air-force Base was about seven or eight miles east of Belleville. People from St. Louis were buying houses in the Belleville area and driving to St. Louis to work. There were freeways being put in. I said, "Lord, is this the place?" The answer came loud and clear "Yes." We rented a house and made the move from Springfield to Belleville.

I joined the carpenter's union. I worked some for Bill, but the Belleville area has a very high water table. About half of the houses have basements and most of them, bad water leaks. The basements were not tiled out properly. I spent the first few months that we were in Belleville drawing plans and repairing water leaks in basements. I could not believe it. But the building contractors said they did not know how to stop the leaks. God's Holy Spirit gave me the wisdom, or knowledge of how to repair them. One house I repaired was actually floating. There was so much water pressure under the basement floor that none of the doors or windows in the house would open or close. After I tiled it out properly the house settled back down and all of the doors and windows closed and opened. I didn't have to repair any of them. God's Holy Spirit was there working for me.

BLOCK #2 said draw some plans and show your ideas to the subdividers. They will subordinate the lots to you. I drew the plans in the evening and weekends. I took the plans and showed them to a couple of subdividers. They were very enthusiastic because they had never seen a 'Storybook House" before. They were quick to say "yes," and that they would subordinate their lots.

BLOCK #3 said call in the subcontractors and ask them to carry their part of the job, such as plumbing, electrical, cabinets, bricks, lumber, and so on. While I continued to draw plans I called in the subcontractors to bid on the plans. They would look at the plans and say "Wow! Those are beautiful! I want to do the work on those houses." Then I would proceed to tell them that they were to carry their part of the job until the house was sold. Most of them would say something like this. **"Why you crazy fool! There ain't nobody gonna do that!"** I would look them straight in the eyes and say, "OH YES THEY WILL. There are subcontractors in this town that will do it."

Now remember, I did not know any of these subcontractors. I only knew our friends Mary Beth and Bill Woods. You see, I knew they would carry me because God's Holy Spirit told me that they would carry their part of the job until the house was sold. The Holy Spirit told me that when I was laying in bed in Brea California and saw the VISION on the wall. When I finished interviewing the subcontractors, including the lumber yards, I had every subcontractor I needed to build the model house, and they were considered to be the most skilled in the area. In the meantime, we asked God to direct us to a corporate attorney. We were directed to Attorney Huber, who handled many contractors. We told him what we had in mind, and that we were from California. He listened to my ideas. Then he said, "are you sure that you know what you are doing?" I said, "why do you ask that?" He said, "there are 11 contractors a month going broke in our area right now. We had another fellow come from California and said he was going to build California design houses. He lasted about eight months. Then he went broke." I said, "Where are those houses?" Luella and I went out to see them. We couldn't believe our eyes. The houses were the design of a house that you would build in the mountains. We incorporated and hired Attorney Huber on a year round retainer. He was our attorney as long as we were in the building business in Belleville Illinois.

BLOCK #4: I incorporated, and as instructed by the Holy Spirit we named the company **"Better Builders, Inc., Designers & Builders of the Storybook Homes."** I was surprised when I found out that no one had even seen or heard of a storybook home, or an early American designed house. No one had ever seen shake shingles on a house, or used bricks, or rough-sawn siding, or three foot overhangs with the rafters exposed, or clipped roofs and much more. (By the way, another fellow built a beautiful early American house in the same track that we built our model home in. He built it on fill dirt and used cheap green lumber. The dirt was not compacted and when it rained the dirt washed away, and the house settled. The green lumber warped and twisted. The house was a mess. I asked him why he did this? He said that other people had *"taken him"* and he wanted to get back at them. I walked away

108

shaking my head. He had gotten *taken* again. We built four more models about five miles east of Belleville, in O'Fallen, Illinois. We advertised on TV and we had over 4,000 people through the models the first weekend that we had them open. I never let the people know who I was. I would just stand around listening to their comments. I let the salesmen take the orders. I overheard one couple commenting about the houses. The young woman said "I don't see why they want to build houses like these. What was good enough for my parents and my grandparents is good enough for me. "THAT DID IT!" They had a brand new Ford sitting out in front of the house. I asked them "Is that your car sitting out there?" They said "yes." I said "wow, it sure is a nice car." They said "yes we like it." I said real loud, so it would startle them, "WHY AREN'T YOU IN A HORSE AND BUGGY LIKE YOUR GRANDPARENTS HAD?" I startled them so much that we built a house for them. He was the son of the Ford Dealer in O'Fallen. I know that the Holy Spirit prompted me to startle them. This was around 1961 or 1962.

I was back in Belleville in another business venture in 1986 and decided to visit some of the storybook homes we had built. At least half of the people were still living in them. I asked them if they had any complaints. Not even one had a complaint. I couldn't believe it. I broke down and cried with joy two different times. I could not hold back the tears. I have never heard of houses being built that long and no one complaining about one thing, especially when the houses were built in sub-zero weather. I might add that I built the houses to the California building code, which is designed to withstand earthquakes.

James 2:26
For as the body without the spirit is dead, so faith
without works is dead also.

Chapter 13

1 John 2:27
But the anointing which ye have received of him abideth in you, and ye need not that any man teach you: but as the same anointing teacheth you of all things, and is truth, and is no lie, and even as it hath taught you, ye shall abide in him.

GENE APPLEGATE

I prayed God would lead me to someone that could draw plans and run my office, because I had to be out in the field training my men on the California production system. I was impressed by the Holy Spirit to contact a friend that lived in Iowa. He was working for a Mobile Home factory installing plumbing. He said he knew nothing about house construction, or drawing plans. I felt that the Holy Spirit was telling me that Gene Applegate was the man for the job. I told Gene that I would teach him, and with the help of the Holy Spirit he could do the job.

Gene had been through Life Bible College in Los Angeles California. The Holy Spirit knew something that Gene and I didn't know, as you will soon see. I helped Gene and his family move from Iowa to Belleville. I started Gene running the office. I then put him on the drafting board, drawing plans. I showed him the key things that he would need to know. He caught on real quick, just like the Holy Spirit impressed on me when He said that Gene was the man for the job.

Gene hadn't been with me long when Rev. Kenneth Erickson from Decatur Foursquare Church contacted us. (Decatur was 125 miles NE of Belleville.) Brother Erickson was expanding his church from a 500 seat church to 1500 seat auditorium. The church was on a corner lot and there was a lot between the church and the education building. Brother Erickson wanted to expand the church over the lot and attach the church to the education building, so it would not look like a remodel job. He said that God had directed him to come to us. He came to the right people. When I did a remodel job I made sure that the job didn't look like a remodel. I showed Gene how to draw the front elevation of the church so it looked like it was the original design. He did a beautiful job. Gene was with "Better Builders" for two or three years and he then went in business for himself. God had a work for Gene to do. He pastored the Foursquare church in South St. Louis, Missouri. He also drew the plans and built the church. He also drew the plans and helped build a Foursquare church campgrounds. I believe he built a church in Colorado, and pastored it as well

So you can see, the Holy Spirit used "Better Builders" to train Gene for the work that God had for him to do.

I thought when I went into the construction business that I had a call on my life to build churches, but evidently God wanted to use me to train Gene Applegate so that he could build churches, and get him into full time ministry.

God did let us do the finish work on the Assembly of God church in Maryville, Illinois. The pastor, Rev. George Ankarlo said that he would ask volunteers to help us. But I said, "no, no, keep everyone out of the way of my men." My men are precision production workers. I sent five men for one day. They put in all the door jambs, hung all the doors, put in all the base and paneling in the church and education buildings, and guest apartment (all in one day!)

My men were good. That is why I paid them 25 cents over union scale. I never had to worry about my men getting complaints about their workmanship. I did not get any. When the pastor announced that all the finish carpentry work was done in one day, you should have heard all the "oh's and oo's." The people could hardly believe it. After church was over they walked around inspecting the work. It was fun listening to the "oh's and oo's."

Mark 11:22-23
And Jesus answering saith unto them, Have faith in God. For verily I say unto you, That whosoever shall say unto this mountain, Be thou removed, and be thou cast into the sea; and shall not doubt in his heart, but shall believe that those things which he saith shall come to pass; he shall have whatsoever he saith.

God wanted Gene Applegate to move mountains. Gene had no idea that God was going to develop a talent in him drawing the plans for churches, building them, and even pastoring some of them. I call that "*moving mountains!*"

Chapter 14

———— ∞ ————

Luke 12:11-12
**And when they bring you unto the synagogues,
and unto magistrates, and powers, take ye no thought
how or what thing ye shall answer, or what ye shall
say: For the Holy Ghost shall teach you in the same
hour what ye ought to say.**

GOING FROM THE FIELD TO THE OFFICE

I now had good and reliable men in the field. I paid the foreman fifty cents per hour over union scale, and the men under him twenty five cents over union scale. When the union business agent found out that I was paying my men over scale he came into my office "ranting and raving." (Like union bosses do!) He said that I could not pay the men over the scale, and he gave me a shove in my own office. He asked "why are you paying the men over scale?" I said it was our profit sharing plan for our men. When I said that, he just stood there and stared at me. Then he turned around and left the office. (A typical union boss!) I was surprised at how I answered him. It could have only been the Holy Spirit speaking through me. I didn't hear from the "B.A." again.

We had so much work, that I had to hire two draftsmen besides myself to draw plans. The two draftsmen said that they had majored in drafting in college, but all they had drawn were cog wheels, so I had to teach them also. We had so much business that we were finishing a house per week.

My father-in-law came to work for me as a Real Estate Broker. Later, Luella, my wife got her Broker's license. She had three salesmen working for her. The Real Estate Company was named **"Colonial Reality, Div. of B.B. Inc."**

Hebrews 10:19
Having therefore, brethren, boldness to enter into the holiest by the blood of Jesus,

Chapter 15

———∞∞∞———

Luke 12:31
...seek ye the kingdom of God; and all these things
shall be added unto you.

THE LOAN COMPANY

I had not been in business long when two men from a Home Loan Company came walking in my office. They said that they had been looking over our houses and felt that they were well constructed, and that their loan company would like to set our building company up on a $250,000 revolving loan. **"Wow!"** We were blown away. The Holy Spirit had been at work for us again. He went *big time*. Thank You, Jesus. I accepted their offer with no strings attached. There were no points, and 6% interest on only the money we borrowed. The going rate for construction money at that time was 10%. We did very much need construction money. It didn't enter my mind to have this kind of money at my fingertips. I don't think we ever exceeded $50,000 in loans, because the subcontractors were carrying us.

By the way, I didn't tell you that when I came from California I brought with me the California building codes, and that was what our houses were built to. That is probably the reason that the houses have weathered the years so well.

Philippians 4:19
...my God shall supply all your need according to his riches in glory by Christ Jesus.

Chapter 16

—∞∞∞—

Philippians 4:19
...my God shall supply all your need according to
his riches in glory by Christ Jesus.

QUEENS PRIDE CABINETS
Div. of B.B. Inc.

My brother in law Rev. Thomas Bozarth and Glena Dell,
my sister were pastoring a church in Browing Illinois.
Browing was about 125 miles north and west of Belleville.
Tom's father had been a contractor in Springfield Illinois,
and Tom was a good finish carpenter. I knew he would be a
good cabinet man.

Browing is on the Illinois river and Browing used to be
the largest inland fishing port in the United States.

I felt the urging of the Holy Spirit to ask Tom if he would
like to build some of our cabinets. He said, "yes, he would
like that." We bought all of the tools that he would need to
build the cabinets, and he was in business. Tom did good
work. Tom and my sister Glena Dell later went on to be
missionaries in the South Pacific islands for many years, with
the Assemblies of God. Their daughter Cina and son in law

Ty Silva are missionaries stationed in the Philippines, and write most of the "Books of Hope" for the Asian Pacific area. Tom and Glena were also the Directors of Teen Challenge in Hawaii.

Colossians 3:23-24
...whatsoever ye do, do it heartily, as to the Lord, and not unto men; Knowing that of the Lord ye shall receive the reward of the inheritance: for ye serve the Lord Christ.

Chapter 17

———∞∞∞———

Joshua 1:3a
Every place that the sole of your foot shall tread
upon, that have I given unto you.

L.M. ROOFING
Div. of B.B. Inc.

The Holy Spirit was urging me to start a roofing company so we could buy direct from the shingle mills. We bought train car loads of wood shake shingles from Canada and the state of Washington. We bought the asphalt shingles from mills in St. Louis, Missouri.

I felt that the Holy Spirit was also wanting me to start a concrete company because of the amount of work that we had. We named that company:

T&B CONCRETE

Div. of B.B. Inc.

G.M. HARDWARE & SUPPLY

Div. of B.B. Inc.

I had contacted some hardware companies and I asked them to send a salesman to our office. I wanted to buy factory direct, but when he came he said they could not sell direct to me because we were not a wholesale company. I said, "come back next week." As soon as he left I put the paper into motion. The next week when he came back we had a hardware supply company. We could now buy direct from the factories. The Holy Spirit was working for us again. I got bold again. I asked the companies to let our company have the hardware on consignment. Thank You, Jesus. They did it. I could hardly keep from shouting right in front of them, (Thank You, Holy Spirit!) because I knew that the Holy Spirit had caused them to react the way that they did.

The companies carried our hardware company on assignment for six months, or until sold. This is hard to believe, but it really happened. We now sold wholesale and retail. Boy, were the hardware stores upset because they had to buy some of their items from us. Where we were paying retail, we were now buying lumber wholesale, and hardware direct from the companies on consignment. Thank You, Jesus! The Holy Spirit was working for me again.

Luke 11:13

If ye then, being evil, know how to give good gifts unto your children: how much more shall your heavenly Father give the Holy Spirit to them that ask him?

Chapter 18

———— ∽∾∽ ————

John 6:63
**It is the spirit that quickeneth; the flesh profiteth
nothing: the words that I speak unto you, they are
spirit, and they are life.**

MY HEART PROBLEM

I had mentioned that I had hurt my heart moving from
California to Illinois. My heart continued to deteriorate.
It got so bad that I could not drive the car. Luella had to drive
me when I would need to go out and inspect the houses. One
day while I was driving I began to feel weak. I told Luella
that she would need to drive. I got out of the car. I started
to walk around to the passenger side of the car, but when I
got in front of the car the life went out of my body. I fell to
the ground. I lay there lifeless for a while. Then life started
coming back into my body.

Later on I was working at the drawing board when our
black house maid came in the office and asked if she could
pray for me. She said (in her southern brogue) "Mr. Miller
could I pray for you?" I said, "why, sure," because I believed
that God would heal me. I believe to this day that that prayer

was the beginning of my healing. I had asked others to pray for me, but now I "got down to business" with God.

I prayed *"Lord, you gave me this beautiful family and Better Builders, but I cannot go on like this. I am trying to be the Christian that Your Word tells me to be. I am trying to be the husband, and best father that I can be. I am trying to be a good employer for my employees. I am paying my tithes and offerings like Your Word says. Lord, I cannot go on like this. Lord, either You are going to heal me, or I am going to die, because starting this day I am going on a fast and I am not going to eat any more until You heal me. If You do not heal me then I will die because I will not eat again until one or the other happens."*

Matthew 17:20-21
Jesus said unto them, Because of your unbelief: for verily I say unto you, If ye have faith as a grain of mustard seed, ye shall say unto this mountain, Remove hence to yonder place; and it shall remove; and nothing shall be impossible unto you. Howbeit this kind goeth not out but by prayer and fasting.

I use these scriptures because I believed that I had a mountain that had to be moved in order to get my heart healed. I wanted God to know that I meant business. I feel that He owned me. I say again. Thank You, Jesus! Thank You Holy Spirit for moving in my behalf again.

It was on a Monday and I had a doctor's appointment the next Monday in Springfield. Luella and I drove up Sunday morning. We attended the Assembly of God Church in Springfield where Rev. George Mandle was pastor. The song service was over and the announcements had been made and Rev. Mandle got up to preach, so I thought. Instead, he said, "I sense that there is someone here that is in dire need of prayer and I want that person to come forward." You notice he said, "I want that person to come forward." There were 100 to 150 people there. I have never been in a church where they prayed for the sick, that some people wouldn't get up and go forward to be prayed for. But no one got up! I didn't think he was referring to me, so I just sat there.

In about a minute or so, a second time he said, "The Lord told me that there is someone here that needs prayer, and I want that person to come forward." No one got up to go forward for payer. I said to the Holy Spirit, "if he says it one more time I will go forward, but if someone else gets up I will come back to my seat."

Well, a third time, but this time he leaned against the pulpit and said, "The Lord definitely spoke to me and said there is someone here that is in dire need of prayer and I am not going to preach until that person comes forward." I got up and went forward and no one else came forward. I was really surprised and I still am. I told the pastor that I had a heart problem. By the way, my brother in law, Rev. Thomas Bozarth was there. He came forward and laid his hand on my shoulder. Rev. Mandle had put anointing oil on two fingers and laid them on my forehead. He then said, **"in the name of Jesus be healed."** That is all he said. At the very time he said that, it felt like someone hit me in the heart with a rock and I shook all over like you would throw a rock in water and the ripples would go out from it, or a charge of electricity hit me in the heart. I don't remember saying anything. I just went back to my seat. The next day I went to the doctor and was examined. The doctor said he could find nothing wrong with me.Luella and I went home rejoicing and praising God. But it didn't end there. Luella started *"sicking"* insurance men onto me. I had to get a letter from my doctor stating what my heart problem was. I gave the insurance companies a copy of the letter. I then kept the original. I have it in my safe. An insurance man came to my office and sold me a "Founders Insurance Policy." "Founder Policies" are sold by new insurance companies. He did not tell me that Luella had sent him to see me. When he came back to deliver the policy he asked me if I had any friends that would like a policy like I was getting. I said they would be a fool if they didn't buy a policy like the one I was getting.

Joshua 1:7b-9
...turn not from it to the right hand or to the left, that thou mayest prosper withersoever thou goest. This book of the law shall not depart out of thy mouth; but thou shalt meditate therein day and night, that thou mayest observe to do according to all that is written therein: for then thou shalt make thy way prosperous, and then thou shalt have good success. Have not I commanded thee? Be strong and of a good courage; be not afraid, neither be thou dismayed: for the LORD THY GOD IS WITH THEE WHITHER SO EVER THOU GOEST.

I feel impressed to tell you about the healing of my right ankle that was sprained around 1950. I was working with another carpenter putting the starter shingles on the roof of a barn, when the ladder run broke and the scaffolding went down with the two of us on it. When I hit the ground I bounced back up. I said, "Wow, that was fun let's do it again!" But the other carpenter was laying on his back and he let out a "bloody" scream. He had broken his back in 3 places.

I took off running for a telephone. I had to run ½ mile to a phone. I don't know whether I sprained my ankle when I fell, or running to the phone. My ankle swelled up like a softball. The doctor couldn't help it.

It stayed swollen and in pain until it was healed in 1982 at a Full Gospel Business Men's house prayer meeting. The leader asked if anyone needed prayer. I said, "Yes, my back is hurting very bad." A school teacher jumped up and said, "let me check the length of your legs." My right leg had always been a little shorter than my left one. I said to myself, "he's not going to *hoodwink* me." I sat up straight in the chair and held myself real firm. He said just what I thought. "Lay your heels in the palm of my hand and we will see what Jesus will do for you." That is absolutely all he said. The calf of my left leg got all numb and my foot started going down past the other foot. I said **"O my, what is happening?"** The school teacher said "Hold still, Jesus isn't through with you yet." Then my right ankle got all numb, and then my feet came in line with each other. The pain and swelling left my ankle. It never has returned. Thank You, Holy Spirit! Thank You, Jesus!

Luke 13:13
...he laid his hands on her: and immediately she was made straight, and glorified God.

127

Chapter 19

———⚹⚹⚹———

Psalm 75:7
But God is the judge: he putteth down one, and setteth up another.

Daniel 2:21
And he changeth the times and the seasons: he removeth kings, and setteth up kings: he giveth wisdom unto the wise, and knowledge to them that know understanding:

THE INSURANCE COMPANY

R emember in the last chapter, I said that when the insurance man delivered my policy he asked me if I had any friends that I thought would like a policy like the one I was getting? I said "they would be a fool not to buy a policy like this." He left without asking me for any names. I thought that was odd. In a few days he came back again and said he came back to make me an offer. He said he would set me up as a General Agent. That meant that I cold sell any place in the state of Illinois, no restrictions. The Founder's Policy commission paid 75% the first year. The Emancipator Policy paid 80% first year commission, 2nd year bought policies 15%, 3rd through 9th years 7 1/2 %, and 2% thereafter. I was blown away. I would receive 25% override on all the men I hired "PLUS-PLUS." The first evening I went out I made almost as much as I did building a house.

I said *"Lord, what is happening? I asked you to help me get started in the building business. That was all I asked, but you have multiplied me with your blessings. Lord, You sent the Holy Spirit to teach me how to draw plans. You gave us a real estate company, a roofing company, a cabinet company, a hardware and supply company. Our companies are supplying everything on assignments. Even the subcontractors and the lumber company are carrying me until the houses are sold. Then You sent the building and loan company in with $250,000 revolving money at 6% only on what was used. The other builders were paying 10% for construction money. You gave me a secretary and bookkeeper that was superior to anything I could have asked for. Iris even estimated my plans accurately. And now this insurance company! It has been lots of hard work, but I have enjoyed every minute of it. Building these beautiful storybook houses and watching the people "ooing" and "awing" and signing their contracts."*

It was 1961. I had houses under contract and agreements with subdividers. I had to do a lot of praying. I needed the Lord's Holy Spirit to talk to me. His blessings were breaking my seams. God wants to bless you if you will bless Him. We were paying 30% in tithes at that time. When I prayed, God and the Holy Spirit said to me, "you have worked hard and I want you to get more enjoyment out of this good life." I said, "OK Lord, I will sell the companies out, which I did."

I started making appointments and signing contracts. I also started hiring salesmen. I hired up to 15 salesmen. There were over 250 salesmen with Land of Lincoln Life Insurance Company. It was easy to sell the Founder Contracts. My agency was in the top 10, or number one, the whole time

I was with the company. If we sold our quota they gave us a summer vacation and a winter vacation in Florida. They gave us the vacation in cash and we always had money left over.

I am telling you these things so you will get some of God's 4000 promises out of the bible, take them before God and His Holy Spirit. Tell Him you are paying your tithes and being the best Christian that you know how to be. I am not wanting to be greedy for myself. I am a hard worker and try to be the best person on the job. God's Holy Spirit will go to work for you just like He has for me.

As time went on they wanted to start a health insurance company. They also wanted to start a holding company so that they could merge the two insurance companies into it. These were stock companies. So, I had to get my security license so I could sell stock for the companies. I studied for the security examination. When I took the exam there were attorneys and school teachers taking the exam with me. Most of the people were well educated. When they graded the papers and passed out the grades you should have heard the swearing. About 1/3 of the class didn't pass the exam. The Holy Spirit breezed this 7th grader right on through.

Oh say, I didn't tell about me taking my Insurance exam. I did not pass it. But the Holy Spirit was there. When the man graded my exam paper and told me I didn't pass, something said to me "stand still and don't say anything." That's what I did. The man then asked me, "what company are you with?" I said, "Land of Lincoln." He said, "Oh, you passed. Go on home and don't worry about it." In a few days my license came through the mail.

Thank You Jesus! Thank You Holy Spirit! He will do the same for you, if you will yield yourself to Him.

They asked me to become an incorporator in the two companies. I accepted. They gave me 10,000 shares of stock. I sold them in nothing flat. I was asked if I would accept a position on the Board of Directors of Midwest Life Insurance Company of Chicago. I said "yes." We later merged Midwest Life Insurance with Abraham Lincoln Life Insurance Company. They later sold Land of Lincoln Life Insurance Company. I then retired from the insurance business with $240,000.

I bought a 1964 ½ Ford Mustang and a 1964 Ford Landau T-Bird. I put over 75,000 miles on each of the cars in one year. I paid $6,500 for the two of them. That is hard to believe, but it is true.

Deuteronomy 11:26-28a

Behold, I set before you this day a blessing and a curse; A blessing, if ye obey the commandments of the LORD your God, which I command you this day: And a curse, if ye will not obey the commandments of the LORD your God

Chapter 20

⸺⛌⸺

Hebrews 13:6
So that we may boldly say, The Lord is my helper,
and I will not fear what man shall do unto me.

THEY CAN'T FIRE YOU
(WHEN YOU ARE A CHRISTIAN AND YOU HAVE
THE HOLY SPIRIT WORKING FOR YOU)

I worked on two jobs where the bosses tried to fire me, but the Holy Spirit would not let them. One was on a grain elevator in a little town outside of Decatur, Illinois. I was a carpenter and I was also the welder on the job. The foreman drank beer for his dinner. When a person like that finds out that you are a Christian they will hate you. I heard the foreman go to the superintendent and give him some phony reason to get me laid off. The superintendent said, "I'm not laying him off. He is too good of a man." They were a traveling elevator company. Their next job was in Kansas City, Kansas. The superintendent asked me to go with them, but I refused because I would not leave my family. I asked one of the men that traveled with the company that was from Texas why he traveled with them? He said he couldn't get a different job. I told him I didn't have a problem getting a job.

133

The next job where the foreman tried to fire me was in Brea California. This was a Bank Computer building. It was the second largest computer relay building in the world, I was told. The building was two stories high and covered almost a whole square block. If the outside electricity failed it had its own built in generator system. I was a carpenter and welder on that job also. My foreman was a Japanese man. I had been there four or five months. He didn't like the way I built some concrete forms, so he went to the office and got my check and fired me. I had built lots of concrete forms. I knew exactly what I was doing, but he didn't. When the superintendent found out that I had been laid off he said "where are you going?" I said "the foreman laid me off." He said, "He's not laying you off. Give me that check and you get back out there to work." The foreman was *mad as hops*, but he couldn't do anything about it. The Holy Spirit was at work for me again.

If you determine in your heart and mind to be the best employee your company has ever had, you will not be laid off and you will make the Holy Spirit PROUD OF YOU.

Proverbs 30:5
So that we may boldly say, The Lord is my helper, and I will not fear what man shall do unto me.

Later on this same job, I was working on some scaffolding that had been illegally built by the laborers. It had twenty foot walking planks that were twisted and not tied down. Another carpenter stepped on the other end of the plank I was standing on and cantilevered me ten feet over to another scaffold. I grabbed the scaffold plank, but it was not tied down either. When I grabbed it, it flopped over. I had on my tool belt, loaded with heavy tools. I was falling on my back to the ground. I don't know how I did it, but I was able to flip over and I landed on my knees in the loose dirt. The Holy Spirit, or an angel had to have flipped me over when I was falling, because it was impossible to have done it with that heavy tool belt on. They called the ambulance and took me to the hospital. There were no broken bones, but I jammed my hips and jarred my intestines real bad.

I took the rest of the day off and came back the next day. The superintendent said I didn't have to work. I could just put in my time. I was sick as a dog. I kept throwing up. They wanted me to go home, but I refused to do it. I did not want to miss work. They sent me to doctors and a chiropractor. At the end of three years of treatments the doctor/chiropractor told me that he had done all he could do for me and that I should prepare myself to be in a wheelchair within six months because of the deterioration in my hips, and lower back.

I pointed my finger at the doctor and said, "You have been working on me for over three years. Now God and I are going to take over." I bought a back swing and a hand sander. God's Holy Spirit helped me find a company that made vinyl pads with foam on the interior that fit the sander. God gave me the right wisdom. I would hang upside down on the back swing and my wife or boy would use the sander vibrator on my back. Within three months I was a new man. Thank You Holy Spirit!

I also received a $16,000 insurance settlement. Thank You Jesus! I think this happened in 1984. It is now over 22 years later and I am still not in a wheelchair. Thank the Lord!

Colossians 2:2b-3
...the acknowledgement of the mystery of God,
and of the Father, and of Christ; In whom are hid all
the treasures of wisdom and knowledge. Amen!

Chapter 21

—⚬⚬⚬—

Malachi 3:8
Will a man rob God? Yet ye have robbed me.

TITHING: A MUST

Tithing is mentioned in the Bible at least 42 times. I have told you in the pages of this book how the Holy Spirit wants to help you get a job and keep it, but if you are not paying your tithes don't expect anything you have read in this book to help you. Throw the book away. God will not bless you.

I've had people say to me, "I don't have enough money to pay my bills *now*. How can I give 10% of my check to the church?!" The reason you don't have enough money is because you are robbing God. Trust me. I have experienced it. Just start paying your 10% tithe and your offerings, and you will soon have money left over. I don't know how the Holy Spirit does it, but it works. When you get your pay check, the first check you write when you pay your bills is your tithing check. Then you pay your other bills. If you pay your bills first, you will not have enough money to pay your tithes. **Trust me.**

Malachi 3:8-10

Will a man rob God? Yet ye have robbed me. But ye say, Wherein have we robbed thee? In tithes and offerings. Ye are cursed with a curse: for ye have robbed me, even this whole nation. Bring ye all the tithes into the storehouse, that there may be meat in mine house, and prove me now herewith, saith the LORD of hosts, if I will not open you the windows of heaven, and pour you out a blessing, that there shall not be room enough to receive it.

Deuteronomy 8:17-19

And thou say in thine heart, My power and the might of mine hand hath gotten me this wealth. But thou shalt remember the LORD thy God: for it is he that giveth thee power to get wealth, that he may establish his covenant which he sware unto thy fathers, as it is this day. And it shall be, if thou do at all forget the LORD thy God, and walk after other gods, and serve them, and worship them, I testify against you this day that ye shall surely perish.

Luke 6:38

Give, and it shall be given unto you; good measure, pressed down, and shaken together, and running over, shall men give into your bosom. For with the same measure that ye mete withal it shall be measured to you again.

God gives life to your tithe money. When you tithe it will reproduce itself. God multiplied the bread and fishes. He will supernaturally multiply for you. God's Holy Spirit will do supernatural things when you tithe.

Hebrews 6:12
That ye be not slothful, but followers of them who through faith and patience inherit the promises.

If you learn to be sensitive to God's Spirit then you will hear His voice.

John 10:27
My sheep hear my voice, and I know them, and they follow me:

Chapter 22

‒‒‒‒⊶⊷⊶‒‒‒‒

Jeremiah 31:3
The LORD hath appeared of old unto me, saying,
Yea, I have loved thee with an everlasting love: there-
fore with lovingkindness have I drawn thee.

THE FIFTEEN YEAR BLIND
DATE THE LOVE STORY

My folks and we children attended a Sunday morning
church service in Decatur Illinois. Rev. Kenneth
Auten was the pastor. The year was 1926. I was five years
old at the time. I was sitting on the front pew by myself. The
pastor's wife brought a pillow with a baby on it and laid
the pillow and baby down beside me. I do not remember
the mother saying anything to me. She then went up on the
platform and played the piano for the church service. That is
all I remember.

I didn't remember that, until the Holy Spirit told me to
write this book and brought all these details to life in my
memory. I truly believe that the Holy Spirit was standing
there and stretching his arms out over that little baby and
myself. I think He said, "I anoint you and seal you two to be
man and wife."

That is all I remember until I was 14 or 15 years of age at an Assembly of God camp meeting at Petersburg, Illinois. I was walking with my mother from our cabin to the camp auditorium. She asked me if I remembered Brother Auten. I said "yes." Mother said, "see that girl over there with those long curls?" I said, "yes." Mother said, "that's Brother Auten's daughter." I remembered the incident because I hated long curls on a girl. Especially since Luella's were all the way down to her hips. I might add that I don't remember ever walking with my mother to the camp auditorium before, or after this incident. I truly believe that the Holy Spirit arranged for me to walk with my mother this one day, so she would point Luella out to me.

About two years went by after that incident. It was the year 1940 at the camp meeting in Petersburg, Illinois. Brother McCorle, the Dean of the Zion Illinois Assembly of God Bible School came up to me and said that John Mansfield was hiring men in Waukegan, Illinois, and I could come and board at his house. I went home with Brother McCorle and got the job. I was working the day shift on December 7th 1941, when the evening shift started coming in saying that Pearl Harbor had been bombed. I worked through the winter and through the summer of 1942. I saved my money and bought a two door, "*hot*" 1936 Ford. It was like new.

Brother McCorle had taken a singing trio during the summer to different churches advertising the bible college. It was now the first of September and he asked the trio to his house for Sunday dinner. There were ten of us around the dinner table. We were all chit-chatting when Brother McCorle spoke up and said, "You know, while we were on our touring trip we met a young lady that is going to make someone a good wife." Now, I was not ready to get married. I still don't know why, but my ears perked up like a horse's does when he hears a strange sound. Brother McCorle went on and on about all of the qualifications that this girl had for being a good wife.

She was a well mannered girl. She played the piano and had a beautiful singing voice, and so forth. I don't know why, except the Holy Spirit prompted me (when he finished talking) to say "you know, if what you are saying is true, she is going to be my wife." Boy, you could have heard a pin drop. It got so quiet. And then everyone burst out laughing and "heehawing." When they got all through laughing and things quieted down, I said again, "If what you say is true she is going to be my wife." Nothing more was said, but I bet they all thought I was a "dumb idiot." He must have mentioned what her name was, but I don't remember him doing that. There was nothing more said about it until I got a letter from my sister.

It was now the first of November and I received a letter from my sister Verna Mae saying that her church was having a going away party for a boy that was going into the army. She said "Remember Brother Auten? Well, his daughter Luella is here and she is going to be at the party, and I would like for you to come down and meet her." "Wow!" I wrote back and said "I'll be there." I asked Willard Bacon to go with me. He was in Bible school there in Zion. He was from our church in Springfield, and a good friend. He later was my best man in our wedding. As Willard and I went into the going away party everyone was sitting on the stairs because the newspaper reporter had just taken their picture for the newspaper. We were too late to get in the picture. As we walked in I saw my sister Verna Mae and Luella sitting together. I was not the type of guy to fall in love with every girl I met, like some men do. But I sure did this time. But I did not let Luella know it because she had just turned fifteen the day before the party. When I met Luella at the party the blind date was over. As time went on and I would be taking Luella out, people would ask, "Gilbert what are you doing, robbing the cradle?" I would always say, "absolutely!" I tried to be just a good friend to her. I always told her "if another boy asks you for a date, go out with him." I remember three boys that asked her for a date several times.

143

One of them went on to be a doctor, but she always turned them down. Verna Mae would confirm this. When you have a jewel you protect it. I have her diary which also confirms the above. Back to the party....

Willard and I took Luella and my sister home from the party. On the way home we went through the middle of town (Springfield.) You should always make a good impression on your girl the first time you take her out, so I stopped right in the middle of the busiest intersection. I then let the engine die. Willard got out of the car waving the American flag, and holding up the traffic all four ways while I lifted the hood up and pretended to work on the engine. We let the traffic pile up all four ways while the girls got excited. We then got in the car, started the engine and drove off. We made our first impression and they never forgot it.

I continued to date Luella and two years later on Valentine's Day I asked her to marry me. She said "yes." I gave her a diamond engagement ring. We got married a month after her eighteenth birthday. In the meantime, I had taken over the family farm and was then a bachelor. We spent our honeymoon on the farm. We were married sixty three years, three months and nine days. The Holy Spirit took her home to be with Jesus, her real lover. I did not begrudge her love for Jesus. I shared my love with him freely.

Jeremiah 31:3b
Yea, I have loved thee with an everlasting love: therefore with lovingkindness have I drawn thee.

Jude 1:24:25 (R.S.V.)
Now to him who is able to keep you from falling and to present you without blemish before the presence of his glory with rejoicing, to the only God, our Savior through Jesus Christ our Lord, be glory, majesty, dominion and authority, before all time and now and forever. Amen.

Chapter 23

LET US WALK IN THE LIGHT

1 John 1:5-10

This then is the message which we have heard of him, and declare unto you, that God is light, and in him is no darkness at all. If we say that we have fellowship with him, and walk in darkness, we lie, and do not the truth: But if we walk in the light, as he is in the light, we have fellowship one with another, and the blood of Jesus Christ his Son cleanseth us from all sin. <u>If we say that we have no sin, we deceive ourselves, and the truth is not in us. If we confess our sins, he is faithful and just to forgive us our sins, and to cleanse us from all unrighteousness. If we say that we have not sinned, we make him a liar, and his word is not in us.</u>

Ephesians 3:20

Now unto him that is able to do exceeding abundantly above all that we ask or think, <u>according to the power that worketh in us,</u>

THE POWER WORKING IN US
IS THE HOLY SPIRIT!

NOW RE-READ THIS BOOK AND APPLY GOD'S PROMISES TO YOUR LIFE.

May God's riches bless you.
Gilbert M. Miller

Printed in the United States
68005LVS00002B/1-201